A SPIRIT HUG

BY

DENISE PILGRIM

Published in 2013 by FeedARead.com Publishing –
Arts Council funded

A CIP catalogue record for this title is available from
the British Library.

INDEX

36 - Stay on the spiritual path
37 - A spirit hug
38 - A spirit kiss
39 - Your happiness is our happiness
40 - I could not stay
41 - I had to go
42 - Do what you feel is right
43 - Go with your instinct
44 - Use your intuition
45 - Don't let anyone use you
47 - It's time to put your foot down
48 - Seek the truth of spirit
49 - Please look after your health
50 - Physical death is not the end but a new beginning
51 - We are sending you healing
52 - You are loved
53 - You have come through the worst, things will get better
54 - Wait a while, it will come
55 - All my love
56 - Try and get more rest
57 - You must relax more
58 - Treat yourself
59 - Life is simple, don't complicate it
60 - Don't think about it, just do it
61 - Try not to worry
62 - Don't dwell on the past
63 - Put your feet up
64 - Remember the good times
65 - I don't have any more pain
66 - I am happy
67 - I still visit you
68 - Keep a positive mind
69 - You are stronger than you think

70 - Let go of the past and close the door on it

71 - Look forward to a brighter future

72 - Things are not as bad as you think

73 - Be patient for just a little longer

74 - Enjoy yourself, have a great time

75 - Live your life, don't let it pass you by

76 - Seek peace and you will find it

77 - Have more faith in yourself

78 - Sit quietly and ask with your heart and soul

79 - Change the way you think

80 - A new door is opening for you

81 - Make your decision

82 - In your heart you know what to do

83 - Don't let your emotions control you

84 - It is time to take control

87 - It is time to express who you really are

88 - Do not hide your talent

89 - Your happiness is all we care about

90 - You are entitled to happiness

91 - A rainbow for you

92 - When you are feeling sad I will lift your spirits

93 - God has not forgotten you

94 - You are here to learn from your mistakes

95 - I speak to you in unexpected ways

96 - Open your eyes as well as your ears

97 - Do not be afraid I come with love

98 - Seek more knowledge and wisdom of spirit

99 - Remember that you are spirit now

100 - Follow your dream and make it a reality

101 - God will not judge you or punish you. He is Love

102 - Your soul is far more important than all the
materials of this world

103 - Take the first step; I will hold your hand

104 - Stay strong

104 - Do not neglect yourself
105 - Continue to speak your truth
106 - Sometimes in your darkest hour you see the light
107 - You cannot change anyone but yourself
108 -Never lose hope
109 - Please do not be angry

FOREWORD

You do not journey through this life alone. You are always accompanied by spirit loved ones and guides whose only desire is to lead you to truth and happiness. The troubles that you endure through life can sometimes consume you causing you to feel as though there is no hope or respite from them, but your loved ones are always with you, wanting to uplift you and console you with their words of love. A Spirit Hug is sometimes needed and with the spirit inspired messages in this book, you can at any time read their words of encouragement when they are needed, bringing you closer to them and receiving the strength to carry on through the adversity that you may sometimes face. There are 100 messages in this book to help you through the coming days. You are not alone but are accompanied by love.

Denise Pilgrim

<u>When I lived on the earth my vision was limited</u>
<u>Now my eyes are wide open and my vision is limitless</u>

Although I lived with physical sight, I now see how blind I was. Many of my actions, I wish that I could now change, but this I cannot do. In all the years that I lived upon the earth, I thought that I was almost invincible. I hardly ever thought about the consequences of the things I did, or of the effects my actions might have on other people, especially those who were closest to me. Rarely did I give a thought about death or the possibility of the survival of death, but now I know, and the knowledge of its truth has indeed now opened my eyes.

Time does heal, even for those in the world of spirit, but the legacy that is left behind on earth, can sometimes take much longer to heal, for memories linger. I now know and I now see the reality, and though I am no longer in the physical body, I feel the pain of those I hurt and that is something that I strive to put right every day. To help eradicate the suffering of others, is my eternal work and forte, and I can never rest until the work is done and I am satisfied that those souls are free from the pain that I helped to cause.

My eyes are wide open now and never again will I close them to the pain and suffering of others, for peace of mind is what every soul deserves, and those whom I still love, I will help at every opportunity without fail.

Please don't be sad. I am with you

When sadness fills your heart and you feel alone,
please know that I am with you.
There are circumstances in your life that occasionally
overwhelm you, and I know that at times you don't
know which way to turn, or who to turn to, but I am
there with you. Turn your thoughts to the memories of
when I was on earth when we would talk things over.
That can still happen. Though I am no longer in the
physical body, I am still with you, and can be with you
in an instant when you send out your thought to me to
help you.
    My love for you has not changed or dissipated, it is
still as strong as ever and stronger still when you are in
need of upliftment. I will be there every time you call
me, without fail, and will support you in all your times
of self doubt. You may not physically see me, but I
will endeavour to make my presence felt in other ways.
You will know. When the simplest thought or memory
of me enters your mind, don't dismiss it, for my
communication with you is easy and gentle and my
love for you continues.
    Just as the gentle breeze upon your face on a
summers day can bring you warmth and comfort, so my
warm embrace can be felt. This moment of sadness
will pass, just as the clouds in the sky come and go.
Gather your strength and we will walk together, side by
side, until you regain your composure and happiness
returns to your life.

Thank you for your prayers - they have helped me

I thank you for every heartfelt prayer that you have uttered for me, and simply because they have come from your heart in truth, they have reached me, and I have felt the love that is within them. At my passing into the world of spirit, the change from living in the physical world to living in the spirit world was one that took some time to get used to, and the separation from my loved ones on earth was at times a lonely experience, even though I was surrounded by those who loved me and had gone before me, but I missed the familiarity of being with those I had left behind and it was initially quite daunting until they taught me what I needed to know about my new place of abode.

Every time you prayed for me, it made the acceptance of my new life a little easier and I was able to feel comforted by your words, even though I felt your grief. I have been to you often and have been able to help you through your feelings of loss, and tried many times to bring my loving influence around you, to let you know of my presence. I am very grateful for your loving thoughts, and want you to remember me in the times when I was thriving in energy, and full of the vigour of life, for that is how I truly am now.

Your prayers of love I now return to you, and I wish you love, peace and happiness in your remaining time on earth, and hope that they will grace each new day from beginning to end.

I am sorry

While living on the earth plane, it is so important to seek knowledge of the world of spirit that becomes the residence for every person that lives. It is not enough, nor does it serve anyone, to say, "Well I didn't know that the spirit world existed", for it will become their home regardless of their knowledge of it. Without this knowledge many people may live selfish lives as I did, thinking that there will be no recompense for their actions one day. It is the gravest of mistakes to live as though tomorrow and the hereafter will never come, or that they do not matter.

This attitude and way of living will only bring sorrow, and sometimes the word; 'sorry' can come too late. "If only I had known", are the words commonly spoken by many in the world of spirit, where ignorance of the facts are realised too late, and with great sadness. There is no clock to turn back here! I can only now try to help those on the earth to this realisation, in a great effort to redeem the life that I lived, and in this way, help to change the world of earth.

My memories, pleasant and unpleasant are never far away from me and I cannot run away from them, but face them, and so it should be, for what would be the purpose of living without learning from your mistakes? I am now humbled by my past actions and greet every new opportunity of helping those whom I have wronged, in the hope that their pain may be eased and short-lived.

Please hold on, there is light at the end of this tunnel

At this time, darkness seems to have descended into your life and all seems bleak. You feel as though you cannot find your way out of your circumstances, and the answers that you seek are not forthcoming. Please do not give up, for your prayers for help have been heard by us and we are trying to help. Although there seems to be no light at all, we are with you. We are working to exert our influence in the right places for a positive outcome. As difficult as it is for you to be positive right now, we ask you to be strong in your endurance as you have been up until now.

In a while you will look back and see how we have guided you out of this tunnel, into the light of understanding. Hold onto your faith which has kept you going. Focus your attention on the light up ahead that is coming into view, this will give you renewed strength to keep moving forward slowly, taking one step at a time. When you feel as though you are about to fall, we will be there to hold you up and will carry you if we have to. You are loved too much by us to abandon you in your time of need, and you have come too far to give up.

We know that you still have strength in reserve to tap into, and this will help you to get through the days that you feel are too hard. You are not alone, and our loving presence and protection will remain with you long after the light returns to your path. In love and light we will always walk with you.

Things are not always what they seem to be

While you live on the earth plane, you should always remember that you are soul and spirit first, and a physical being second. Your soul existed long before your material body was created, making you a spiritual being first and foremost. While in the body you are limited by your physical sight, for the eyes of the spirit can see much further and deeper than your physical eyes can see and it takes practice to see clearly. Every circumstance of your life has a spiritual theme and thread running through it, that you usually miss because you look at what is presented to you in a material way.

The spiritual truth of the situation is usually overlooked, because it lies beneath the surface. If you learn to look at matters with a deeper understanding, using your spiritual knowledge, you would not be so overwhelmed by circumstances that often cause you so much sadness, and they wouldn't appear to be such a trial in most cases. It is usually with hindsight that your troubles become clearer and the hurdle appears not so high and you are heard to say, "If only I had realised that at the time, I wouldn't have worried so much". Once the problem has past, you seem to have much clearer sight, but during the troubled time your sight becomes clouded by the circumstances.

Forgive yourself, release the guilt and move forward

Please do not hold on any longer to the feelings of guilt that you have carried like a heavy stone for too long. It weighs heavy on your heart, preventing you from truly moving forward with your life. As a spiritual being, you were created to make progress which suggests movement and flow, but a river cannot flow freely if there is a structure built across it causing an obstruction, and if the water is still it will cause it to stagnate. Every day is a new day to make new decisions and to live by them, but if you continue to live in the shadows of decisions made yesteryear, then you are not really living.

It is time to call a truce. Make the decision to accept that an action or a decision may have been made in error, and made at a time when you were learning and growing as you still are and ever will be, and forgive yourself, for striving to be perfect is not something that you will ever stop doing, and neither is making errors of judgement. You have since that time, made many decisions that have fairly tipped the balance in your favour and caused that moment to be of no consequence, but still you feel you must bring your past with you to live in the present.

In this moment, please know that you have not been judged or found guilty by those who love you in spirit, but we urge you to let go and live in the knowledge that your future happiness is being built and prepared by today's actions. Please now step out of the shadows into the sunshine without fear.

I am with you still

I have not gone, I am with you still and that has never changed since the day that I left the earth. In death I changed from a soul expressing myself through a physical body, to a soul expressing myself through a spirit body and I now have no restrictions of time or love. Please do not mourn for me, but remember me with the same love and tender thoughts that you had for me when I was physically with you. In time your pain will subside and your feelings of loss will be replaced with pleasant memories, for we shared many good times that can never be erased.

We were at times one, in harmony with each others thoughts and desires and I assure you that that will never change. We are still one, for every time you think of me, I am right by your side. Every time you recall past events that we shared, I am there sharing them with you again. You must not doubt that life is truly everlasting and eternal, for I tell you life does not truly begin until you cross that threshold called death, and what a word of false pretense is that word, for in many it instils so much fear, when in reality it is a kiss of liberation from the pains and troubles of a material world.

Love never dies and my love for you has multiplied with each passing day, as I sit not at the Father's right hand, but at life's eternal table of progress and happiness.

I love you more than you know

When living in the physical body, we try very hard to express our feelings to one another, using words as a tool. Sometimes this is successful, but many times it is rather substandard, and words can fail to give vent to what is trying to be expressed. Many times on the earth I felt that words had let me down, and so on occasions it was better to say nothing, for always those I loved I took great pains not to hurt. But now that I am in the world of spirit, it is much easier and words are no longer a barrier against expression, and to communicate sentiments without words is now a moment by moment occurrence.

Love is the most powerful feeling in all the world, material and spiritual, and its power has always surpassed words, even in the physical world, and this I wish to bring to you now, by saying that you are loved more than you know. You are at a slight disadvantage being in a material body, for it dims the spiritual senses for the time that you dwell upon the earth, but I tell you now that one day you shall truly know the depth of the feeling of this love, and you will then understand why love in its expression on earth, pales so much against its reality of expression here.

There are not enough words in your dictionary that can give love enough credit, but my heart and soul have no trouble actively loving you more than you can now know or understand.

When you think of me, I am with you

I am never far away from you. On the material world of earth the term, being close to you, is usually spoken of in physical terms. Here in the spirit world the mind is more alive and mobile than it was ever possible to be on earth. Thoughts are more real and are not just cloudy wisps that evaporate from the mind, they have form, and whenever you think a meaningful thought about those you love in the spirit world, we receive them just like a telephone call, but even quicker. As your thought is formed it is received by us and we can, in the time it takes for you to finish that thought, be with you, for your love always draws us to you.

I have spent many tender moments with you, sharing your thoughts and memories and in this way, reliving the good times with you from our shared past. In this way we communicate, as I exchange memories with you. Often you will remember something from the past that you may not have thought of for years, and suddenly there you are remembering something you thought you had forgotten. The pleasurable memories of the past are what we hang on to here, and to revisit them with our loved ones on earth brings us great joy and happiness always.

The joy of living is an eternal asset, and when it is shared even in memory, its upliftment permeates both worlds.

<u>Dry your tears, I have not gone</u>

How can I convince you that I have not gone? How can I tell you that I stand by your side, when you cry and mourn for my loss? When I left my physical body behind on earth, it was just the shell that I rose from. That shell was just for a short time, the covering and temporary home for the real me, my spirit. My spirit body continued to live, truly live, for I now inhabit a beautiful world to which you too will come one day and inhabit. I wait for you with longing, knowing that this longing will one day end in a joyous reunion.

Life is not truly life until you leave the physical world, for all that you desire and wish for in terms of what you would like to accomplish, can be yours here. When you cry for me, it saddens me to know that you feel apart from me, but this is not the truth for we are still together even though we are on different sides of the veil. I still hear you, so continue to speak to me. I still see you and walk with you sharing your experiences. I hug you when you need comforting and I continue to try to help your awareness of my presence to grow. I may be gone from your physical sight, but your spiritual sight and senses know that I am with you still. Let them work for you, do not stifle them, and in this way you will again enjoy our partnership and friendship on a much higher level that death cannot erase.

My love for you is stronger now than it ever was

When I tell you that my love for you is now stronger than it ever was, these to you are just words, but behind these words lay a depth of feeling of which you are not accustomed to on earth. When you live in the material world, words are often spoken that do not belie the truth of what is being felt and experienced at the time, and how can they? Words are a weak portrayal of heart and soul expression.

In the life that I now live, words do not have to be used. We communicate our truth without them, and are understood without further explanation. I visit you often and I see the troubles of your mind, and the heartache that you sometimes have to go through just to get through life. These occasions and experiences, I go through with you in the sense that I feel your different emotions, and because of my love for you I also feel your pains and your turmoil as you try your best to live your life and deal with the different problems that arise. I remember my own experiences and this causes me to be filled with admiration for your efforts, because I know how hard it can be, and I do not say this in a trivial way. I know.

The time will come when we will meet again, and then my true feelings of love will be felt by you in all their glorified beauty, but until then I have to use the words of a language which does not do true justice to the words of love that I bring to you now, and are everlasting in their heartfelt meaning.

I walk with you

Many people who live upon the earth, think that they are alone. There are times in their lives when they are overwhelmed by earthly problems and struggles, and they have no one to turn to for help, such is the physical life. There are even times when help is asked for but forthcoming it is not, for more and more people are living insular lives where, to reach out to others is seen as being weak in nature, but you are never alone. You cannot see the spirit of the loved one, now living in a spiritual world, who is by your side. You cannot see the many helpers whom you have called out to for help, surrounding you in your time of need, giving you strength and trying their best to comfort you.

I am not alone when I quickly come to your assistance in your troubled times, for often I bring with me those that you know and those that you don't know, but we are all of the same mind and intention, to bear you up and guide you along until you find your way again. I walk with you at times when you are happy, sad and indifferent, but always my intention and desire is to let you know that your journey through your life is not a lonely one, but one that is walked with friends and family passed and present.

There is nothing to forgive

There are many times in life when actions speak louder than words. These are the times when you are called to perform some feat without thinking, but behind the action is a clarity of heartfelt expression which words cannot explain, but it is clear to everyone what was meant at the time. At these times thought was not involved, but the senses were in play, working, in hindsight, for the greatest good of all concerned. On these rare occasions there may not have been an opportunity to explain oneself to those involved and the occasion may have passed by and the events soon forgotten.

Once the parties involved arrive in the world of spirit, it is clear to see that the heart and soul were working together in harmony, and that is love in action. From the spirit side of life, there is no longer a physical body to hinder our sight and therefore there is nothing to forgive, for we can see the reasons behind everything that is done and all is made clear. We do not need explanations for the things that you do, for we see the reasons before you do the things that you do, and your motivations are to us loud and clear.

For every action there is a reaction. For every cause there is an effect and the law of love interpenetrates them all. Do not spend your time regretting the things that you have done or not done, for all will eventually work out to your advantage in the lesson called life.

In time we will be together again, but for now live your life

When I passed into the world of spirit, I did not close the door on us. We share many happy memories of which I still revisit with you. Those memories will for me always remain active and alive, and I feel your concerns sometimes when you wonder if I still feel the same love for you as I did when I was on earth. That love I assure you will never change or lessen in any way, and for the time that you continue on the earth plane, it can and will only grow in its value and intensity, for we remain as one.

It is important for you to realise that although I am not far away from you, I am continuing my life in another plane of existence not too far removed from yours, and I know that in time, we will be together again. Time is of little consequence here and although your longing for our togetherness continues to be felt by me, I can still be with you as you continue to live your earthly life, for as long as that may be.

Life on earth is always a little harder to bear when a loved one passes over, and that pain and loss is by no means one sided remaining with the loved ones on earth, the emotion is felt on both sides of the veil by all concerned, but time passes by and slowly heals causing the appearance of that divide to get smaller.
Togetherness of the heart can and does cross any gulf whether physical or spiritual in its being, and as long as you have this knowledge and understanding, your path will be made easier when loss and the grief that comes with it is experienced.

You are never alone

On earth when we were together we shared many moments of joy and laughter. There were also times of sadness and occasions when just being in each others company was enough to bring us contentment. The ups and downs of life were made easier because we shared our lives living as one unit. We became for each other a sounding board of complete trust, which saw us through every problem and difficulty that we encountered, but for you that seemed to change when I left.

We knew that one day one of us would be left behind as the other made that journey to the other side of life, but we did not discuss this journey that we all one day make. Had we done so the preparation of mind for the one left behind would have been done and the transition from earth life to spirit life would have been one of acceptance and pleasant expectancy rather than reluctance. Now that I am here in my spiritual home, I know that life continues beyond the physical plane of existence and still I come to you to share my news as I always did, that has not changed, for it is information that you often wonder about and a truth that you often hope for.

You truly are never alone, for when I tell you that I am with you always, I speak words not of fantasy or false hope, but words of loving truth, a truth made clear once the door to eternal life was opened to me, and to all those whom you have loved but never lost, for in death we found life that breathes happiness and contentment.

Make that change, I will help you

Life is filled with opportunities that seem to wait behind closed doors, until one day our curiosity gets the better of us and we open that door to see what lies behind it. On these occasions we sometimes wonder why this new opportunity was not discovered by us sooner, such is the ease at which we find ourselves embracing it. It is not that we didn't see this door of opportunity before, but that the familiarity of seeing that same door every day failed to arouse within us any wonder about its being there.

We enjoy and get comfortable with the things that we see and cope with every day, until we become bored with the same surroundings. There will then begin to stir within, a certain wanting for change, caused by the need for growth and new things to experience. This is where you are now, you are growing out of your old and familiar spiritual clothing, the ones that you have held on to for so long but have now outgrown.

I am here to help you to make that change, to knock on this new door of opportunity which is about to be opened for you because the time is right. With confidence and the tenacity to take this new step, I will walk with you helping you through your moments of uncertainty. Do no worry, for change in everything and in everybody is the essence of new growth, and in that growth lies the presence of the future which is yours to embrace.

Pray and the answer will come

There are times in our lives, when we just cannot do things alone and we need help. The Divine Father did not send us to this earth to walk our paths in loneliness and solitude. He provided us with companions of spirit to accompany us and it is up to us to make use of these spirit friends who willingly offer to lead us and guide us on our spiritual pathways. As souls treading this earthly path we frequently lose our way and require the occasional helping hand, from a loving guide who can point the way, giving us direction when we are lost.

If ever we need direction, it is when we are at our most vulnerable with no earthly friend to say, "I have your total interest at heart and wish nothing in return", for these are the expressions of love given to us by our unseen but present guardians. They work not just for us, but ultimately for the Divine Creator who has instilled within them the deepest desire to aid those who have lost their way and are temporarily in darkness. You do not take them away from any important work when you ask in prayer for their help, for you are their work, done with love and commitment to the Divine Father.

When no other option is available to you and you have tried your utmost in every way to solve your problem, then open your heart and pray for the answer, it will come in the most unexpected way, and your thanks will be heard and accepted with heartfelt love and joy for the service rendered to you, freely and unconditionally.

Yes, I was with you

There have been so many times when you wished that I was with you, and I was there. There have been times when you yearned for my presence in a moment of sadness, and I longed for your awareness of me to be such that you no longer doubted my presence by your side. On occasions you have momentarily thought that your imagination played tricks with your mind, but no, I was there. In a moment of silent tears you thought you felt a gentle touch, but quickly dismissed it as fantasy of the past bringing cruel hope to the present moment of desire. But if only I could erase your doubts, and increase the awareness that you struggle to hold onto, and sometimes deny, then there would be no more tears of loss and grief, for you would know and never wonder if it could possibly be.

In the time that has gone by since my passing out of this world, and entering the spiritual world, I have rarely left your side. For you the time has been long and heavy on your heart, but it is not a true reflection. I am no more gone from your life than have your memories of me, for I know that they have never left you and that they visit you daily as do I, and when my memories cease it will be because we have reunited beyond the grave of earth and are creating a new future together, with a new life which has the eternity of time on our side. I am with you always.

Yes or No?

There are many times in life when you find yourself in a dilemma when it comes to making decisions of importance. There are occasions when action needs to be taken and you have to decide on whether the answer to your question is yes or no, or should I or shouldn't I? It is difficult, especially when your decision will affect those closest to you in some way, for whatever decision that you make, some will agree with you and some will not, some will be happy and some will be sad by the result of your decision, and to you that is the most important part, because hurting others by your actions is not something that you take lightly or ever intentionally do, and so your heart in a spiritual way, is involved.

When you find yourself in this place and moment of your life, take a look deeply within yourself. You know that your intention and your motive is never to hurt another, and whatever road you take in making your decision, your hope is that it will ultimately be the best outcome for all those involved. If your loved ones know you as well as we in spirit know you, they will realise this.

Promise yourself that when you cast the dice of opportunity, you will follow your heart's decision, for it is your heart that will see the correct answer and will become at odds with your head when it tries to interfere. The mind is a mirror image of the heart, a reflection, and it can sometimes distort what it sees, which is not always a clear picture.

Push open the door to your heart and peep inside, there you will find your answer and your true guidance.

Take your time, do not rush

In the world of spirit, the one thing we have plenty of is time. Indeed there is no time except the present. There is no rising and setting of the sun as it is on the earth to denote days, and there is no clock to watch and measure time as you know it. There is just perpetual light which is warm and comforting, much like your summer days.

When you have a job to do or an event to take part in, you have to complete it within a certain time scale, for you only have a certain amount of hours of daylight in which to perform your duties and tasks, so it is understandable that you get into the habit of rushing through your day and attempting to finish your tasks within a time frame that suits your needs. But at what cost do you rush? You can see, but you do not see, you can hear, but you do not hear and you touch and feel things but do you really sense them? All the senses given to you are hardly used to their full capacity. The jobs that you do daily are skimmed through at speed, without you taking the time to connect with their inner teachings and meaning. You always want to jump to the next task when you hardly remember the previous one.

Beware of rushing through life in a dream-like state. Appreciate every small thing that you do by being present in it, and then you can say that you got the most out of your day. Your time on earth is short compared to eternity in the spirit world. Wake up and live each moment, don't rush, for on earth time is an illusion that disappears in the blink of an eye, but if you truly live, then you can capture every moment before it disappears into the past.

Sometimes mistakes are a blessing

When things go wrong in your life due to an action that you have taken, you call it a mistake, even though at the time you did what you did, it seemed right and was done with the right intentions and motives. The outcome of your action may not have been what you expected it to be, and this may have brought disappointment to you as you deemed it to be the wrong result. Your disappointment may be real and you may even feel guilty about the action that you took originally, but you cannot always see the truth of that outcome. You may feel that the result was a negative one, not the one that you expected, but there were others involved whom you could not see.

The circle of involvement of those affected by your original action was much wider than you could see, and they may have gained something positive from your mistake. Someone somewhere on the outskirts of that ripple effect, received something of great use and value to them and they knew not from where it came or how. Your sight is limited and you do not always see the bigger picture, and this you should learn to accept, for when you look back on this life on earth you will one day see how your connections with others stretched further than your eyes could see. You touch people seemingly unconnected to you in many surprising ways, so never be too downhearted by the mistakes that you make, for your mistake is another person's gain even though you may never meet.

You are more appreciated than you know

There are times in your life, when you feel that you are of little help or benefit to those around you, and sometimes you wonder if you are worthy of being in the lives of others or even if there is any benefit at all to your being here. At these times when your thoughts are beginning to take this tone, I would like you to stop and think about how you got here. Think about where you were several years ago, before you even knew the people whose lives you now share your life with.

They did not know you or your life before you met, and when you did enter each others lives, there were positive changes on both sides. The experiences that you all shared have brought changes in the way that you each see people and view the world. You have learnt something from each other. When you entered into their lives, dark times seemed a little brighter for them, even if you think they didn't show their gratitude. Personalities were uplifted and changed, even if it was only slightly, as you perceive it to be, and this because of your presence in their lives.

A rainbow stretches from one end of the sky to the other, and all those underneath it can look up and see it from wherever they are standing and in the same way, you have touched many who have encountered your presence, even in the smallest of ways.

You are appreciated more than you know and what is more important, is that your appreciation shown for others, has gained you love and respect from a crowd of unseen and loving friends who surround you in light from the world of spirit.

Try to stay calm

In the rush of life it can be very difficult to remain calm and poised. You tend to forget that you are a free spirit born of love and peace, and that these attributes are actually a part of you. It does you no good spiritually to become irritated during your daily activities and it disturbs your wellbeing when it becomes habitual.

Remember how as a small child you were not disturbed by the activities of those around you. You observed and you just carried on with your gentle way, prepared for whatever appeared on the horizon for you and dealing with it as it came along. Yes you were only a child, but from child to adult, you have forgotten how you naturally embraced peace and things that created an atmosphere of calm. This you need to learn again.

It is one thing to be an adult and to get caught up in the adult life and world, but if this does not serve your purpose of living in the now, then you would do well to learn to connect with that child again, who has not left you but is merely quiet.

Become again the child of the past who is in fact a great teacher of how to endure the fast pace of life and remember to breathe in the quietude once in a while. You are not a train rushing through life to get to your next destination, but are a simple being of love created to experience the journey of life and absorb the good qualities that life has to offer you. Do not miss them.

You are on the right path

When I lived on the earth plane, I continually searched for light, not the physical light that surrounds you each new day, but the spiritual light that shines upon the pathway of life that you journey along. This light which is called truth, was lacking in my material life, but I still knew that there was something that I wasn't quite seeing or understanding.

My path was long and sometimes rocky, but I now know that if I had listened to the internal guidance that we all receive, my life would have been less dark at times and progress of a spiritual nature would have been more rapid. I now see as I have never seen before, due to the falling away of the blinkers that accompanied me through life. I tell you that you are far more privileged now to know the truths that have been afforded and taught to you, for the path that you now follow is the right one which will lead you to a much brighter destination than was mine.

Progress is yours to make if you continue along the road that you have chosen, for you have listened and acted upon the direction that has been given to you. There is only brightness in your future, and you will one day recall the moments when you acknowledged the voice of reason within you, and kept your free will on an even keel as you steered your life through the waters of endless events and opportunities. You will always be guided by love.

In time you will understand why

The material life is one that is lived by action and reaction, cause and effect. In our daily lives we are prompted to carry out many deeds that prove to be right for us and sometimes we feel that our actions have brought the wrong outcomes for us. Nevertheless we are beings and creatures of habit. It is not wrong for us to react to what we see and feel, for we were all created with senses that guide us through our lives, and help us in many ways, but occasionally our reactions are so extreme as to be without sense or feeling for those who are closest to us. We neglect to be sensible to their feelings and this we do constantly through life, but not deliberately.

It happens that one day our lives will change, and all that we do, say and think will one day be remembered and recalled in their entirety, and when this day comes through the occasion of death, our works on the earth plane are understood, with a reasoning that was difficult to use when we were in the body of flesh. There are many who regret their actions while living on the earth, but they are not judged by any Godly entity for the laws of cause and effect do their work effectively.

Every why that you ask will one day be answered in a manner of clarity that will satisfy your craving for the truth. Until that day comes, please continue to live your truth in the best way that you can so that peace of heart and mind can be yours eternally.

Be a little kinder to yourself

This is not a perfect world that you live in, and neither have you yet reached perfection. You have a long way to go before you become completely satisfied with yourself as a spiritual being. It is not for you to judge yourself as being unworthy of others' kind attention to you, for what do you know of their needs? You do not know their inner feelings, for these you cannot see or always understand. They do not always express themselves in a way that you can see or even comprehend, so what right do you have to feel unworthy of their love or of their time?

You are a child of The Divine Creator who once created a soul of tender loving care that is expressed in so many ways by you. You do not shout about this talent that you have for caring about others, because you do not need to, it is seen and recognised as a trait of love within you by others, you may not see it within yourself, but we certainly see it from the world of love that exists beyond your physical eyes.

We have learned that those who shout the least and live their lives quietly trying not to get in the way of others, are the ones who need our love and assistance the most, for their hearts are larger than they would seem to be and they do not take the credit for the work that they do for others. Your kindness to others, we recognise. Please allow yourself this compliment.

The truth will be revealed

When living on the earth plane, enlightenment can be hard to achieve. If the mind is not open to truth because of indoctrinated teaching since birth, it is hard for truth to be accepted when it is presented to you. The mind can easily be directed and moulded along certain lines of thought which shut out the light of truth if it is not sought for during the earthly span of life.

As with all truth it is eventually found, and all things hidden are eventually brought out into the light of realisation. There are also times during your life when earthly truths are hidden as opposed to spiritual truth. On earth the mind can hide certain information that should be shared with others, and for various reasons decisions are made to keep the facts from those whose interest in them are not seen as being important enough for their revelation to take place. But all things in the fullness of time are seen clearly whether on earth or after passing out of the earth. It is easy to hide true feelings and thoughts in the material world, but in the spirit world there can be no such evasive practices. There is never the entertainment of falsehood in the spirit world for all is based on truth. Your mind is always in a state of flux and you should be aware of the intentions of those who try to keep you in the dark with regards to truth. Use your intuition always so that the truth of all things cannot evade your detection.

Stay on the spiritual path

This journey upon the earth is only for a time, and whether it be short or long it will one day come to an end only to continue in another place where time does not count. The pathway that you take on your physical life's journey is important and this many people do not fully understand. The path you are now on is one that you have been guided to take by your loved ones in the world of spirit who care deeply about your spiritual wellbeing, as well as your physical wellbeing, and this is why you have embarked upon this search for spiritual truth and sustenance. You have become tired of what is considered to be the acceptable way of searching and accepting truth.

You have become a leader rather than a follower, in that you have decided to take up the reins of your own mind leading you in a direction that is far more revealing of who you truly are. Not all that you seek to know is written in a book of historical value that can no longer be relied upon as spiritual, for spirit cannot be found locked away within either pages or bricks and mortar.

The spirit of life surrounds us all, we breathe it every day and it cannot be contained, for it is far too powerful. Look beyond the physical for your answers and the spiritual path that you walk will lead you home to the destination of truth that you seek. You will be guided.

A spirit hug

Oh, if only you knew the depth of love that we in the world of spirit feel for our loved ones on earth, you would never again feel unloved in any way. You cannot capture by the use of mere words the truth of feelings that are expressed by us towards you daily. We see the heartache and the suffering that you sometimes experience. We feel the pain of all your struggles and we can do nothing but come around you with our deep sympathy, for these experiences we too have suffered at some time.

Humanity as a whole is suffering, mostly caused by their own actions and lack of love for their fellow man. Selfishness has taken hold of individuals and has spread as they try to reciprocate rather than forgive and attempt to rise above its escalation. We know that the souls of many call out in the darkness, feeling empty sometimes of care for others or even themselves, and even then we bring our love to bear upon them, hoping that our presence can be felt and that the situations of torment can be assuaged.

Let us all come together and be the shining light and example of love which brings warmth to all hearts. This we can all do as individuals on both sides of the veil. We can all play our part making even the slightest difference to one who is in need, which counts as a hug of contentment.

We cannot always prevent man from hurting each other, but when you are hurting, we love you all the more in our attempts to soothe your pains.

A spirit kiss

When peace enters your heart, even for a moment, you must know that you have entered momentarily into the heart and domain of your Creator. It is a moment when the veil between the two worlds has been drawn aside causing them both to merge, and you have been privileged to feel the kiss of the eternal law of love. These are moments that you should seek and when you find them, treasure the experience.

You are at the helm of your ship, which sails through this material life, you can at any time find these moments when the physical life can be left behind with all its misery that sometimes engulfs you. Be the light that tries so hard to break through the darkness, and when you succeed in achieving this you will know that we are all one. The heart can then beat in rhythm with the Divine and all that it has to offer. The true colours within that surrounding light, can then shine in all their glory, and bring to you the happiness that you deserve and seek.

When that gentle breeze blows across your cheek and yet the wind is still, a kiss from your loved one in spirit has been given, but it is not just a kiss from heaven, but it is a kiss from all those known and unknown to you, who wish to make their presence felt. They are but a glance away from you, present at all times of loving celebration when they share in your achievements. They do not abandon you, but come ever closer to bring you their love. Acknowledge and accept it with grace.

Your happiness is our happiness

There is nothing that uplifts us more than to see you happy. Life on the earth plane is scattered with its ups and downs, and we are with you through them all, but our hearts sing when you meet your achievements, celebrate your anniversaries and enjoy your family gatherings. We join you at all these times and our hearts sing with yours on these occasions. What is life for if it cannot be enjoyed to the full?

We thank you always when you bring joy to others and uplift their spirits, for that is also part of the work that we do whenever we can. A smile on your face puts a smile in our hearts too and this is a gift that should be shared with all. Far too often hearts are made heavy with the more serious parts of life, and the monotony of making a living can get in the way, but life is too great a gift for it to be constantly about surviving, and all those things that lend themselves to striving to get through each day. You will always survive, and one of the greatest gifts worth celebrating and pondering is eternal life beyond the physical grave.

Celebrate often those things that bring you joy. Take the time when you can to include those who rarely have the same opportunities that you have, and make every moment possible a time to remember in a positive light, for memories are precious and happy ones are priceless.

I could not stay

I know that there have been many moments when you have asked why I had to leave. You have asked this question and wondered if things had been a little different; would the outcome of my leaving the earth life have been the same? I have been with you when you have shed tears for my departure from the physical life, and I have heard your wishes for me to be back with you again, but I could not stay.

The laws that govern death have to be obeyed, and they are not put in place to hurt the ones we love. My leaving the earth is a law that we all one day have to embrace and succumb to. It is not a punishment but a release from the ties of earth and all its circumstances, and is more liberating than you know. I am constantly by your side wishing that your sorrow could but evaporate with the knowledge of the truth of death. There will be a time for us to meet again in the world of spirit, and if only your awareness of me was such that you could know that I am with you, all your doubts would flee in an instant and would be replaced by a more satisfying acceptance.

Put aside all your fears about my whereabouts for I have not gone far or gone forever, and when we meet again at the appointed time, there will be only joy in our reunion and continued life will be ours to enjoy again together, with harmony and love as our constant friend and guide.

I had to go

On the day that I left this earth plane through the door called death, I know that you shed many tears for me and I saw and felt your grief. You could not understand why, neither could you bring yourself to accept it for a long time, but it was my time to leave. You prayed that I might stay, you were even angry at my departure, but I understood your feelings.

The laws of death apply to all. When the physical body cannot sustain life any longer, the spirit leaves the body. There is a time to be born and a time to exit the physical world, and the length of time spent on earth is different for everyone depending on many circumstances. The physical body is just the temporary vehicle for the soul and the spirit, and life on earth for however long or short it may be, fulfils its purpose of giving life to each as an individual. After that time life continues on another plane of existence, but it is truly life nevertheless.

I have become even closer to you now, even though you may not be aware, but its truth whether known or unknown to you does not deter my continued love and companionship with you. I am still the same person that you knew and loved.

Please know and understand that I still walk with you, sit with you, cry and laugh with you. Our parting is only temporary, as though called away only to meet up again in the future. Dry your tears and know that eternal life is a friend to us all.

Do what you feel is right

At the end of my life on earth, I was able to look back through my memories and see the results of all the actions that I took. I was able to see clearly how my decisions affected all those close to me and understand my true motives for doing the things that I did. There were times when I was motivated by love, sometimes anger and there were times when I knew that my actions were not the right ones to take.

When making your decisions it is important that they are made with heartfelt motives that feel right. Often we are challenged in that we have to battle with our conscience and on those occasions, our guiding conscience should be listened to, for it is the voice of reason which should not be silenced. Only you are responsible for your own actions, and for this reason it is a great responsibility when deciding how to act. Your intention and motive is everything and as long as they are honourable in your decision making you need have nothing to fear.

You will never please everyone around you, since they all have their own life agendas to deal with and these you do not have responsibility for.

Bring yourself to a place of mental stillness and begin by listening to yourself, for at the back of all of your decisions are your desires, and as long as they are for the highest good you will always be guided by love.

Go with your instinct

There have been times I know when you have been at a loss about what to do in certain situations. You have found yourself faced with a problem that has caused you to wonder which way to turn in making your decision. There were many possible avenues that you could have taken at these times, and when you knew that others would be affected it would always tug at your heart making the problem more delicate to deal with.

There is within you a place that especially deals with these occasions and within that place lies the instinct which is always at work, provided that it is not overlaid by materialistic thoughts and actions that tend to make its workings less automatic. This place of instinct lies within us all, and it can be recognised by the fact that it does not question but has a knowing. This instinct knows the answers before they are asked and can lead you to places of safety where thinking cannot take you. This is a gift that can only increase in its power and quality the more that it is used, and you should trust it. Without it you are as a lost sheep wandering aimlessly through life, but if you learn to listen and act upon it, it can save you many hours of discomfort and turmoil in your life.

Begin to recognise when it is working, it is your greatest friend and people who have learned to rely on it have seen wondrous life changes that would normally not be attained without its use. As with all gifts, it should be used wisely and in good faith.

Use you intuition

There have been many times in my lifetime on earth, when I was given to some quite reckless behaviour, which was usually regretted in the moment after it was performed. Regrets are many when you come to the time of looking back at your life and seeing the many errors that were made, sometimes in the heat of the moment. There are of course just as many occasions when the right action was taken in balance, but at the time no reason could be given in explanation for it, and it was said that at that time I was out of my mind and that is a very good way of describing the intuition.

It is a form of taking oneself out of the mind and using just the will. It is able to overcome all sorts of barriers that are raised between you and the object of your desire to overcome. You know how to use it, for as a child you depended on it to get things that you wanted, either from difficult places or from people that you did not know well. You worked it in a way that allowed you to be uppermost in your intelligence and frankly accomplished your goal without any fear. Nothing has changed, for you are still the same person that you were then, but with more life experience now. Do not let that life experience hinder your intuition from working for you.

Bring to the fore intuition's powerful disposition of making light of every situation that you think may be difficult, for it is only a thought. Move past that negative thought and feel the correct and right way to go. You already know it and have therefore already achieved your goal.

Don't let anyone use you

Remember that you are a single minded spirit with the strength of endurance that cannot be compromised by another who feels that they may have dominance over you. You have within you an awareness that is working all the time, especially when you come across those in life who wish to take advantage of your kindness. Be kind always, but be strong of mind so that those who are week in their spiritual navigation of life cannot tread upon you. They mistake your spiritual nature for weakness, but they have no understanding of spiritual things and you can teach them about self conduct.

You are not a follower but should seek to lead those who have lost their way and do not see others as their equal. Allow no one to use you for their own ends, for this is a time in your life when you are ready to fly above the pettiness of those who seek to deceive. You hold a unique passport of spiritual intent, which should not be given over to others who do not know how to use it. Be your own person at all times. You have come too far and have been through too much to allow your self- worth to be taken from you by one who has chosen to walk a different pathway to yours. Keep your own counsel and your own belief that who you are now has been achieved by many experiences that have been the price paid for your loyalty to goodness and decency.

It's time to put your foot down

There were times in my life on earth, when those that I trusted were the ones that hurt me the most. They were the ones whose friendship I treasured and sought for companionship to ease my way through life. Life is not easy on the earth and many a time we all need consoling in one way or another through our troubled times, but without inner strength which we all have but do not always use until it is too late, we can cause our own fall to take place while putting our trust in those whom we hoped were friends.

There is a time to make a stand for yourself and state your truth of who you are and of who you are not, and when this is done with truth and honesty you will always be heard. You do not have to be arrogant or in any way distasteful, but when you need to be heard for the sake of what is right, do it with strength and force so that your voice is unmistakeable above the din of those who do not see your true being. There will be as a result, a clearing of mistaken identity or falsehood and the road will be one made easier to travel along without diversion in the minds of all those concerned.

Strengthen your resolve to make amends to those who did not understand your nature or stature at the beginning, for they will know who you truly are as long as you continue to be clear in the statements that you make.

Seek the truth of spirit

Since coming to the world of spirit, my eyes have been opened spiritually and truthfully. My years spent upon the earth were not without its trials as you have experienced from time to time, and there are truths which I am now in possession of that I wish I had knowledge of when I lived on the earth.

The dark times that I endured, I felt were put upon me at times by some great outside force that was in control of my life, and this was my great mistake in thinking. I now know that there are laws both spiritual and physical that govern us all when living a material existence, and these I was ignorant of greatly to my chagrin. Now that I am in possession of spiritual truth, I feel that it is my duty to instil these truths into the minds of those I love upon the earth, in order that their lives remaining on earth can be made better and with less troublesome effects to their lives.

Spirit and all the truths that allocate themselves to its truth are not myths, neither are they difficult to learn, but are by their very nature simple understandings and when put into practice, bring love in many aspects to the hearts of all who walk and seek the path of spiritual light. Do not waste your life looking for only material knowledge, for beneath them lie the spiritual truths that are needed for your soul's growth. Life and growth are synonymous with your true being when sought with a spiritual flair.

Please look after your health

It is not worth ignoring your own health in the pursuit of assisting others to maintain theirs. You are required to be strong, and for this to happen you must see that you can only continue to perpetuate your caring for others when your own health is in tact. Please know that to disregard your own state of health and being would cause, in the long run, much distress to others who appreciate you in a much greater way than your belief will allow you to think.

You are living in a physical body which requires maintenance through the correct and useful intake of sustenance, and without it the spirit within cannot function to its greatest capacity, for its expression can only take place through the physical body. The two are needed to work together in harmony and if this harmony is disturbed, then the natural workings cannot continue. Breathe in fully the light that surrounds you, both physical and spiritual, so that you can continue your path of bringing happiness and joy to those you love and serve. Be not of the mind that these things can take care of themselves, for without the efforts of your physical body and spiritual counterpart you cannot survive the journey of earth. You are needed to function at your best. Please extend your mind to your physical and your spiritual wellbeing. Both are important for a balanced life.

Physical death is not the end but a new beginning

To live your life with the constant fear of death overhanging your life is not truly living but is debilitating in its cause. It is not an ending by any means but is a transition from one life to another which is greater in every conceivable way.

It is a natural part of life such as birth, for in physical death which accompanies all to a world of life and progress, you will know and understand the true meaning of living. Put aside all your fears, for they are due to misunderstandings acquainted with finality, and the reality is that there can never be finality as long as there is a Creator, for in creating life He created continuous change in all aspects of life. Life changes from one aspect of life to another and in this there can be no end. Truly live each day without fear and for the betterment of your soul and spirit, and in this way you will eternally become the true being with the purpose fulfilled that you were created for.

Death and all the falsehood of finality attached to it will one day become the spectre that it is, for its false teaching and bringer of fear will evaporate in the moment of its occurrence, becoming a welcome friend and a teacher of many truths previously unavailable through lack of spiritual direction while on earth.

Live each day with the thought and promise of a future beyond this earth plane, a future that you are creating in each moment that you enter and embrace with your thoughts and deeds.

We are sending you healing

Our love for you is such, that whenever you are experiencing emotionally hard times there is an outpouring of love and healing towards you and all those involved in your situation. We are constantly telling you that you do not endure these moments of sadness alone, and this is a truth that we always try to instil upon your troubled minds.

Love is not just a word that is bandied about without thought here in the world of spirit, but it is a real power with the ability to heal wounds and become as though they were never opened in pain. When you doubt our ability to do this it makes it a little more difficult for you to receive it, for to receive you must be open minded enough to reach a place of calm that ensures the healing can be effective. During the storm when all is dark and the strong winds of the earth are blowing, the sunshine would hardly be noticed because of the elements that have gathered up action. Please know that we are reaching out to you at this time and in all times of sadness and low energy, when you are tired and feel that you cannot go on, faltering in your steps.

Love blows away the cobwebs of despair, and we know that our efforts are not in vain when we see you coming out of the darkness of that tunnel of experience, that you entered unwillingly because of your circumstances. We bring you new hope whenever we can, in the form of countless messages of a healing nature, that rise up in your mind when we draw close and embrace you with our love and upliftment. Be open and receive.

You are loved

If only you could see the loved ones that surround you on a daily basis, you would never doubt our love for you. You think that you are alone in this world of physical life, but that is not so. You have many friends and relatives of the spiritual nature, that you no longer see since they departed this physical world, but never has this been a barrier for their continued expressions of love.

They come to you when you call out their names in despair, for their concerns for your wellbeing did not die with them. When on the earth they were called for help, there was never any hesitation in that help forthcoming to you, but still you doubt as to whether their continued love for you is real. It is real, more real than you could ever know, and at this time of your life it is essential that this realisation should come to you, for it has never been more important for you to know this truth. If you begin by realising that love can never die but increases in its power and being, then you can move forward in your grief and loneliness.

You cannot be alone or without spiritual aid at any time, for to be so would be against the laws of spirit which are all encompassing, meaning that they stretch across the bridge of death where love can come and go unabated and it is through this love that we work to bring to all souls the love that heals and works to unravel the hurts and pains of life. You are loved!

<u>You have come through the worst, things will get better</u>

We know that there are days in your life when you encounter feelings of sadness and depression, and these are times when you feel that the darkness that surrounds you will never lift and give way to the light, but I promise you that that is not so. You struggle at times I know, to lift your head above the waters that drag you down with the strong undercurrent of unrest that your soul sometimes experiences.

Life is all about change, and from one day to the next you can feel vast differences in your emotions, but I tell you that if you can find that strength within and fight the negative thoughts that engulf you occasionally, we will do all that we can to lift you up. When you call out in your pain and your sorrow, you will see that shaft of light begin to break through your darkness in ways that you cannot fathom or even expect. You have come far along the road of troubled times and I promise you that this cloud of uncertainty will lift. Trust and have faith in that power that is greater than you or I, it does not pass you by when you are at your lowest ebb, but carries you along to the shores of comfort.

You have come through the worst and even though you feel it will never end, the end is in sight. You cannot see how far you have come but we can see how far you have to go and as you enter the final phase of your troubles, we guide each step that you take, and as heavy as they are, they are leading you to calmer waters and happier times.

Wait a while it will come

You live in a world full of expectancy, a world where you expect all of your desires to be fulfilled. It is good to have hope and this you should never lose for without hope life would be tragic in many ways. In many circumstances we in the world of spirit push the boundaries as much as we can to help you, but we have to work within the laws that govern us all.

There are times when we would happily take on your problems and your troubles, shouldering them to prevent you from feeling their pain, but this we cannot do. We suffer the agony of watching and seeing the struggles that you go through to achieve the things that you desire, but it builds your strength. Knowing what we now know and seeing the results of your actions long before you embark upon them, we know that at times it is not right for you to have all the things that you want when you want them, and you do not always know what is good for you. Be patient. Always learn to bide your time, it is a gift you would be wise to understand.

The phrase, 'all in good time', is a truth few people understand, for there are reasons for all occurrences and a time for each step in the process of acquiring the things you want and need. Place yourself at the mercy of the powers that guide your life, for they are more intelligent and wise than you think. All good things come to those who wait. These are words wise beyond your knowledge and understanding, but one day will become clear when you will see the 'whys' and the 'wherefores' of everything in your life.

All my love

Love is not material, nor does it desire material things. It is of the heart and of the spirit. The truth that it holds within it is not of the earth for it transcends all things physical. When love enters your heart it colours everything that you do with different shades of happiness and can always be felt by those who receive its magical strength in emotional upliftment. It can change the face of every event when perceived as the true friend that it is, with its great strength.

On the earth, to give love is noble when given truly from the heart, but in the spirit world it can be shared and given as the true gift that it is, without any pretence of feeling and in its pure state. I give to you all of my love, for that is what we were all created to give. I cannot be in any other state of mind than the one I present to you now, for to be so would not express what I am to you or the love that I feel for you. Since love is an expression of life, then why not give it as often as you can. It can be demonstrated in so many ways but as long as that demonstration is from the depths of your being, it will always be the golden thread that runs through the lives of all those living on both sides of the veil.

Please know that my love for you has not changed or left my soul, for it is in permanent residence within me and has not lessened in its intensity or feeling. When we meet again you will understand this truth and for all time, you will be in its warm embrace with the continued desire to share it with all those you meet.

Try and get more rest

You try so hard to please so many that you tend to neglect your own needs. It is of course admirable that you constantly have the needs of others on your mind and that their attention and needs are to the forefront of your duties, but this will not bring you the desired rest that you need. It is time for you to put aside some time for yourself. Take the time to treat yourself occasionally to the same pleasantries that you freely give in service to others.

You are I know determined to make the lives of others much easier to bear by the giving of your time, and I know that you teach by example the need to put others first without thinking too much of the self, and this you have done with true zest, but when you are tired you must listen to your body and do not push it to its limit. Try now to get the balance that is needed. Your work is greatly appreciated and you of all people must not deny yourself the same privileges that you give to others.

You have great strength within and your spiritual strength is seen by all whose lives you have touched, but occasionally take a back seat and let others drive so that you can enjoy the journey and not miss the wonderful scenery that passes you by. Slow down a little more and the strength that you conserve, you can use for the enjoyment of life's panoramic views which are there for you to see and appreciate too.

You must relax more

The material world is full of anxieties and things that cause you to constantly feel on edge. Your mind is always thinking ahead of the moment that you are in and hardly ever has the opportunity to just be still. When you think of relaxation you tend to think of the body being inactive, but this is not enough, neither does it give understanding to its full meaning.

The body can be perfectly still but not at complete rest if the mind is still churning, for if the mind is in a state of anxiety giving thought to things that cause it to be in a state of alert, then the body must follow suit because it takes its instructions from the mind. If on the other hand your mind is calm and being filled with thoughts of a nature that are serene, then the body will react accordingly. You seem to spend more time on the thought treadmill than you do on the lake of peace and then wonder why your body is stressed and full of knots!

You owe it to yourself to occasionally become an arbitrator for a more peaceful frame of mind, and in that I mean to picture yourself as one who is free from the trammels of life that try to prevent you from being the true epitome of calm and quiet. In this state your awareness of life and the beauties it offers you everyday will increase and you will never get bored of seeing them but will seek them wondering how you never noticed them before. Take the time to breathe and relaxation will take on a whole new personality undeniably pleasant to experience.

Treat yourself

Sometimes you can get so bogged down with living that it becomes very serious and unfulfilling. Each day can feel the same as the next in its repeated way of doing things. It becomes a continuous treadmill of daily events which threaten to bring no variety or upliftment to you causing a melancholy state of being within. It is at these times that you need to think of ways in which you can break this thread of monotony.

The spirit within thrives on new experiences that bring a lightness to your demeanour and a positive change to your outlook on life. There may have been times in your life when while you were travelling to a certain venue, you mistakenly took a wrong turn which turned out to be the greatest and most scenic wrong turn you have ever made, bringing joy to your heart as you observed the sights laid out before you. This would have been such a positive experience for you that the next time you were making that particular journey you sought out that same route, even though it took longer to reach your destination. That would have been described as a treat worth having because of the way it lifted your spirits.

The same attitude should be adopted during your daily life. Find a way to treat yourself in a way that will bring you happiness in even the smallest of ways, for these little pockets of joy in your life, can be the difference between the enjoyment that life can offer and the lows of continuous and deepening depression and sadness. Live your life!

Life is simple – don't complicate it

We in the world of spirit, often watch our loved ones on the earth as they live their daily lives, dealing with different situations that occur. In many ways we see how the simplest of actions required are sometimes complicated by your reactions to them. You know most of the time how you should proceed in your dealings with the many people that you meet along your pathway, and yet when the moment comes you fleetingly get into a mode of thinking that completely changes the outcome of the situation. After the event, which is now completely different to how you envisaged it prior to your dealing with it, you can see clearly how you should have acted or handled your part.

In a moment of disassociation from your true self, you have found yourself on a pathway that you did not intend to be on and certainly did not plan to be walking along. At these times we do our best to exert our loving influences upon you and those concerned to get you all back on track but it is not always easy since your free will cannot be encroached upon by us. Life is simpler than you think. If you use the laws of give and take, that simple exchange of respect for each other, life would not be so complicated.

We know that life is not all plain sailing but we do know that the simplicity of doing unto others as you would have them do unto you, has always worked in favour of harmony. Live simply and love simply, it will bring light into your life and into the world.

Don't think about it, just do it

There were many times in my life when I had ideas about things that I wanted to do. These were things that I knew would benefit me and others in different ways, and that I knew would change my life. I would spend many hours thinking over my ideas and living them in my head. I always waited for the right time, but for many of these wonderful ambitions, the right time never came.

It saddens me now that I let the material world get in the way, preventing me from fulfilling many of my dreams, for there was never any real reason that I can see now, for not carrying them out. Oh the times I spent procrastinating and wondering 'if'! If this happens first then I can go ahead. If that happens then I can do what I need to do. If I get this, that or the other it will help, but all to no avail. There were many times when the opportunity did present itself, maybe not in exactly the right measure that I would have liked, but they were stepping stones towards my desired goal which I did not recognise at the time.

Take opportunities as they come along, don't miss the boat then regret not boarding when it docked for that short time. Yes it is good to make your plans, but sometimes they have to be altered to fit in with the utensils that you have at the time. The greatest adventures in life come about by taking chances, not reckless ones, but those that are guided and helped along by us every step of the way, as long as they are motivated by positive and good intentions, the outcome of which will bring harmony and upliftment to both yourself and to others. Don't be afraid to put your ideas into action.

Try not to worry

I know that there are many things going on in your life at the moment which are causing you a lot of concern, concern not just for yourself but for the wellbeing of others in your life. It is hard, I know, for you to raise your mind and thinking above these worries but you must try. The cause of your worry is such that you may not see it come to fruition. It may be that you have been given the wrong information, but you must consider your wellbeing. Please try not to ponder so strongly upon this tiresome problem for it is wearing you down. I do not say these things because I do not understand, for I do, and I also know the effect and stress that it is having on your physical being.

At times I try my best to soothe your troubled mind, but it is awash with doubt and fear and it makes it difficult for me to draw close to you and help, making you feel as though you are alone. You are not. I place my hand upon your brow often, attempting to bring you the healing that you need for your mind to become peaceful. We try our best at times like this to help as much as we can, and I hope you know that we see the reason for your actions and understand them, but please try to take as many moments as you can to distract your mind with other things, so that your worries will recede in their strength and control over you.

You will soon see that you need not have worried so much, and the light will go on in this dark time helping you to see more clearly and to lessen your turmoil. We are all with you.

Don't dwell on the past

Please take for yourself some credit for the things you have done in your life to bring happiness and joy to the lives of others. You seem to find it much easier to dwell on your perceived failings. This is not a correct assessment of your achievements and you do not deserve to treat yourself in this way.

Life has a way of leading us all to different points that teach us many things, important lessons that are needed to build up strength within us. There is not one person on the earth who can say with truth, that they did not regret an action or a word spoken out of turn to another, and those regrets may have been valid, but those occasions taught them something valuable and that value has carried them through the rest of their lives with a little more wisdom added to their mettle. It does no good to constantly dwell in the past. The lessons of the past have already been learned and there is no need to constantly revisit them.

The present and your future are what are now the most important; they are what you can now control by your thoughts and actions. Be kinder to yourself. You have a job to do, in that your life and all the changes that you can make today will have pleasant repercussions if you start with a positive mind and outlook. Build your future, don't look back.

Put your feet up

There are many times when I watch you rushing around, trying to get everything done in the short space of time that you call, the day. You try very hard to please many people and feel obligated by the senseless rule of finishing the chores and other engagements in a time frame that does not allow for you to stop, breathe, and rest. Your determination and drive to do everything is admirable, but you must know how wearing this way of life is on the body. You then crash unconscious the minute that you sit down and let go of your adrenalin filled mind and body, only to start again with even more aggressive and feverish delivery caused by a feeling of guilt due to your very temporary moment of respite.

This way of life is not giving any quality to your life. When you stop and take some time for yourself during your day, it should be meaningful and deliberate. You should not feel guilty about having moments to recharge your energy levels for they are necessary to your wellbeing, both physically and mentally. When you are burnt out from physical stress it will be much more difficult for you to return to your normal state of health, as catching up takes a lot longer in the healing process.

Please be kind to yourself and rest when you can. The benefits to you will be greater than you realise, and your strength can be retained for those moments when you are called upon to exercise those greater requirements and responsibilities. Rest and recuperation should be welcomed into your life and not forced, so that the time spent in the healing quiet can be used to revitalise your strength and spirit.

Remember the good times

I know that you often think back to the past reminiscing about events that took place and in some ways changed your life. You do though, tend to revisit the times of stress and sadness a little too often, which has little benefit for you in your present life. We are all shaped by our past and there are occurrences there that are better left in the darkness of your memory, rather than constantly reliving them and bringing them back to life.

Your happiness is always my concern and it is when you are happy that you get the most out of life and are able to enjoy your life now in the present. Think more of the happy moments and the good times that you experienced, for you can still learn from them and by your wistful revisits you can again have the same moments of joy, even though they may be through nostalgic memories. We both shared those happy times, and I often walk with you down memory lane to those pivotal moments in our lives, when the experiences and their true meaning have stayed with us, causing our hearts to rejoice in a way that cannot be repeated. We can take strength from those past events in the way they have positively affected us, though they are now historical occurrences that caused time to stand still for us at the time.

Those happy times of the past seem brighter and more vivid in their place in history, but although they are the past, remember that they are there for you to enjoy as often as you like and care to engage in their reflection, bringing nostalgic upliftment to the present.

I don't have any more pain

The memories of my last days spent on the earth in discomfort or pain have now faded. My physical body was closing down and had deteriorated to the point where it was letting go of the physical life. It had done its job of being host to my spirit body within it, and it could no longer function in the way that it did when I was in the prime of my life. This to you I know was distressing to witness, and I know that you worried greatly for me and wanted my pain to cease, and with my physical death it did. I left my material body of flesh behind, with all the discomforts that it held and when I took my last breath on earth, my spirit body, perfect in every way, rose out of its shell leaving it behind for ever.

I no longer have any of the earthly pains that afflicted my physical body and they are now just distant memories. I now live a full life without the mental or physical pains that I experienced, and can truly say that I am alive and well. You must not constantly remember me as I was in my final days of illness, for it is not the condition that I am in now. My happiness is now full and content, and I would not wish to be represented by those memories of sadness, which you occasionally revisit. Please remember me as I was when I was more vigorously able and physically well, for those memories are closer to my present wellbeing, which is life in every meaning of the word. I live!

I am happy

You often wonder about where I am, and about what I am doing since I left the earth plane. When you have these thoughts and wish that we could engage in conversation again, I am usually right there with you, by your side listening to your many questions and following your thoughts of the past. We walk together down memory lane, although you may not be aware of my presence with you. I am as close to you as I ever was and I assure you that I am happy in my new life.

The life that I lived on earth has little comparison now to the life that I live. I now know what living truly means. I now see more clearly than I ever could on earth for I am no longer limited or confined to a heavy material body. I can be in any place that I desire to be in an instant, for my thoughts carry me there. I can learn anything I wish to learn, and all those things that prevented me from fulfilling my desires on earth no longer hinder me and I am free to pursue them.

On earth the physical body is slow and dense, but my spirit body is light and does not limit me in any way. I learn new things in a fraction of the time that I could when on earth, and my thirst for knowledge has increased a thousand fold. Freedom now has a whole new meaning and truth, and I absorb and feel the beauties around me in a way that enables me to blend with them. Happiness is indeed mine to enjoy and yours to look forward to in the fullness of time. I am very happy!

I still visit you

When I passed away from the earth at my death, I was very aware of the sorrow felt by my loved ones remaining on the earth, and I was also present with you during your time of grieving for my departure. When you cried I was with you and tried my best to comfort you, knowing that my presence could not be seen or felt. It is a sad fact that those on earth who do not have the knowledge of survival of death, have to go through this rather traumatic time of grieving for the loss of a loved one, when in fact there are many occasions when the one being grieved for is in attendance at most of the family gatherings that take place thereafter.

My love for you all at these times is even greater because of the pain and sorrow felt by those who feel that their loved ones who are laid to rest are gone forever, and my greatest wish is that all will seek and find the truth of life's continuation beyond the grave. The sorrow would be eased somewhat although the grief for the lack of physical companionship is understood, as is the sadness. But it is by no means the end, for I visit you and am with you constantly in mind and in spirit presence.

I wish that you would acknowledge and increase your sense of awareness and recognise the feelings that you ignore when I am present with you. There are times when you wonder if it is possible that I am with you at certain moments in your day, and at those times I almost rejoice at our reunion even though it is clouded by your doubt. Yes, I still visit you.

Keep a positive mind

Life on earth can be hard indeed with all the trials and ups and downs that it presents. It can be plain sailing one day and stormy seas on the next, but always these difficulties are temporary, even though you cannot always see when they will end. They can cause your mood to change and cause you to become quite morose as you tackle these times of darkness.

You have been given many tools to help you to deal with these troubled times, and if you use them daily they can see you through the worst of these trials. Hope is not just an empty meaningless word; it is one that can help you through the most turbulent of occasions when it is held on to. There is always hope, and it should be held in the forefront of your mind at all times as a guiding light to the ship in trouble on the dark stormy seas. Without hope there are no possibilities of improvement in any situation and you cannot always see beyond the dark clouds that you are engulfed in. It gives you an instant positive outlook that may not be found without hope being your chaperone.

A positive thought will always help when you feel you are being buffeted by life, and when these thoughts are continuous they will arm you against any harmful doubts which threaten to bring you down. Keep a positive mind and raise yourself above life's temporary setbacks, so that you can see more clearly the path that lies before you.

You are stronger than you think

There have been many times in your life when you thought that you would not survive a certain situation. You were so engulfed in the process and constantly thought of its negative aspects, that fear became your master and clouded your vision for a short time, but you still survived and lived to tell the tale today.

At some point in your problem of such colossus size, you found the strength to carry on, taking one step at a time. Each fear was proved wrong, and was flung by the wayside bringing you through the darkness into the light of calmer and sunnier times. What was it that brought you through? Your own strength and will to carry on was your saving grace. You were not even sure where it came from, but you held on to that strength calling on it when it was needed the most. You can use that same strength now, for it has not abandoned you, it is a limitless well to be drawn upon whenever the need for it arises.

That well of strength can never run dry, for each time it is used it is replenished with a better quality of strength for its next perusal. Trust in yourself, and the help that you will always receive in recognising your ability to overcome, will help you to persevere and eliminate your doubts about your capabilities. You are far stronger than any negative thought your mind can fabricate, for positive thought is the light and strength that stems from love, the greatest power of all.

Let go of the past and close the door on it

When you allow yourself to constantly dwell in the past you prevent yourself from moving forward achieving your full potential. You cause yourself to mark time and stand still preventing your own self development. There is a need for you to embrace all that is new in your life; to arm you for the future bringing you renewed strength.

Take every opportunity to deal with what is on your plate now and the desserts of future happier times will follow. When your thoughts of an unpleasant past that you do not care to be repeated come into your mind, send them to where they belong, behind the closed door. Do not allow them to encroach upon your present happiness, for by doing so you give them the power that they do not deserve. In your younger years you were a different individual compared to the strong minded person that you are now, and that strength you can now use to shape your destiny, becoming a better calibre of person than any past events could produce.

There is a saying that you should look at how far you have come, rather than to look how far you have to go, and this you should do every time you begin to doubt your self worth in any way. Your future achievements, though not yet accomplished, should now be your focus and these you should look forward to for they are a part of the new individual to be created by you and you alone. Every step you take is accompanied and guided by love, and with this knowledge, there is no need to dwell in the past.

Look forward to a brighter future

If only you could see ahead to your future, you would realise that you need have no fear. When you desire all things positive in your life, this creates a ripple of positive energy through your thoughts and these go before you as you walk your path. It is so important to keep your thoughts free from any negative persuasion as they can infect your actions without you barely noticing it taking place. Keep your head high at all times and your thoughts above the line of demarcation which draws the line of distinction between hope and listless action.

I have seen your capabilities and I know that you can break through any barriers that are put in your way, so the future that you are creating for yourself is one of perfect standing for you as you require it to be. That is not to say that you will not learn valuable lessons along the way, for those lessons are a part of every life and aid us all to become wiser in the process. Try with all your might to become the person that you wish to be, the person that you envisage being in that future picture that you hold within your mind's eye, and walk and work towards it. If it is right for you it will begin to take shape sooner than you think, and the wisdom that you gain along the way will shine within you in that future that you are holding and shaping in your hands.

Things are not as bad as you think

There are times when it is difficult to be positive due to the circumstances that are surrounding you, especially when each day seems to be a struggle. You endure situations that are sometimes quite painful and you wonder if you have the strength to carry on, but you do, and you find that strength from a source deep within your soul which helps you to face another day with a little more hope in your heart that things will get better.

You have no idea of what the next day will bring, and this is a frightening prospect which you learn to deal with in the best way that you can, and nothing more is expected of you, for when you put your faith in the greater powers that be, you can be helped to achieve your desires and the better things in life which help you to prosper spiritually. It is rarely the case that the things you build up your fears about, ever happen in the way that you imagine they will. You then give a sigh of relief and say to yourself that you worried for nothing. It was indeed wasted energy on your part, for the fear that you felt so strongly, blotted out your reasoning and logic for a short time.

Try to see each new situation as it should be seen, as a new opportunity for you to experience something that can enrich your soul, giving it the opportunity to express its latent gifts which it otherwise would not bring to the surface, to use in a show of strength. Positive thought will dilute those harboured fears, which can be turned into a show of strength allowing you to have the self control that you need.

Be patient for just a little longer

At times you are very frustrated that the changes you desire do not come into your life when you want them. In the material life you frequently ask and pray for things which you receive when the time is right and when the conditions are right for you to have them, and your patience for these things is worthy of praise, for you are in general a person of great perseverance even in difficult situations.

You have within you the gift of seeing the reality of circumstances that others may not perceive in the same way, and often you are required to encourage and guide others in such a way that they are caused to refrain from making rash decisions or mistakes as a result. There are occasions when your endurance begins to weaken, and these are the times when we in our most loving way try to bring you the strength that you require, so as to ensure that you do not feel alone in your time of need, and this we do with compassion for you and a desire to see you succeed.

We ask you at this time to persevere for a little bit longer, for we know that you have been feeling a little abandoned and are floundering at this stage of pursuance of a better future for yourself. Your patience will be rewarded as it always is, and we do not abandon those we love when they experience hard times, but continue to work all the harder to bring about the positive results and outcomes that you seek. Do not give up, we are with you.

Enjoy yourself, have a great time

The trials of life on earth can sometimes weigh heavily upon the heart, causing you to become unhappy and serious about the life that you live. When the problems of life become monotonous and serial like, it is easy to forget that life is to be enjoyed. The Creator created all souls to be happy, and it was never His intention that the troubles of the world should be taken upon your shoulders causing you to be in a place of constant sadness, and this you should remember so that every opportunity for respite from your worries is taken when possible.

Every opportunity that is presented to you that brings a less intense experience of the world, should be taken so that upliftment and forgetfulness of your woes can help you to move into a place of happiness, even if it is temporary, for then you can experience the other side of the coin - the enjoyment of life through positive and happy experiences.

All that is positive should be brought into the arena of your life, to help you to share your soul's potential of giving and receiving. Seek the light of enjoyment whenever you can, darkness and gloom are not the right conditions for any soul to grow in, and when your mood is lifted you are then able to express your true spirit. Live life and enjoy it! Feed your soul with the richness that the enjoyment of life brings and all those around you will benefit too.

Live your life; don't let it pass you by

You have within you the great capacity to live your life to the full, with all the experiences it has to offer on a daily basis. You cannot expect to journey through your whole life on earth living it for others, without gaining anything of its joys for yourself. You are important as a spiritual being and you must sometimes take the chance of doing things that will bring you the many delights of spiritual as well as the physical enjoyments.

This physical life is only for a short time, even if you live into advanced years in material terms, and the lessons during that time are of course many, but to allow the years to pass you by for an idle cause is one that will cause you regret. Try to experience new ideas and new ventures, so that they will instil a fresh zest for life, which will bring you many new lessons and teach you things about your own abilities helping you to progress spiritually.

To tap into new possibilities and achieve things which you thought were impossible within yourself is a way of ensuring that spiritual growth can take place and for the soul to express its innate qualities. Take the opportunities to truly live your life, and bring yourself to the door of new experiences whenever you can, so that your testimony of life will be one of tried and tested spiritual gains.

Seek peace and you will find it

While living in the material world, it is often hard not to get carried along by the fast pace of life that it encourages you to keep up with. You tend to live in a never ending rush with your mind always one step ahead of what you are doing, planning and living in the future rather than living in the present. When the mind is in constant turmoil about the next event in your life, peace of mind evades you causing your body also to follow the same pattern of living, never being at ease or relaxed.

There are times when you ask for just a little peace, just a moment in your day when you have nothing to think about or to cause you any angst, so that the worries of your world do not invade your peaceful state and can stay behind the firmly closed door for a time. You tend to forget that you are in control and are capable of setting conditions for yourself that will aid the peace that you seek. Do not allow yourself to be carried along by the fast running waters of life. Find for yourself those small oasis moments when you can become you and connect with the deeper and more valuable parts of your spiritual self, and there you will find your sanctuary.

The peace that you seek for those brief moments in your day will offer you the strength and respite that you need to carry on. It is up to you to take it. You owe yourself a little peace, the medicinal benefits of which will only improve your spiritual health and help you to find within yourself and your day, a small haven and window of comfort well deserved.

Have more faith in yourself

When times are hard with troubles of both an emotional and material nature, it is the time when you need the most support. We in the spirit world are never far away from you and at these times in your life, we draw ever closer bringing with us our love and encouragement for your problems to be resolved. We help in the best way that we can, and will always try to bring our loving and calming influence to bear upon all those involved in your situation, so that a positive outcome will come about.

We know that you struggle sometimes with the decisions of varying kinds that need to be made, and it is with these decisions that we will try to help you with, for we know that your self belief becomes weakened when the emotions are stirred. You must remember that every decision that is made in good faith, and with the motive of increasing the wellbeing of yourself and others, does not have to be pondered about for great lengths of time, or with any fear.

When you are trying to decide on the best course of action to take, and how to overcome your difficulties, make your decision knowing that you are being guided and helped. Your instincts are your best guide, and the help you to know that your heart is involved in the process. In that moment your faith in yourself and in the spiritual aspect of love, becomes your strength. Use that strength to help you to move forward in the belief and knowledge that the present and future are in your control, but that you receive assistance from us when it is asked for.

Sit quietly and ask with your heart and soul

You are used to discussing problems with others, and this can often help you to come to a conclusion about how you should act in a given situation. You will get the opinions or advice of others which will help you to weigh up the pros and cons, helping you to decide on which action you should take; but there are times when this course of action may not be suitable, when it concerns matters of the heart or matters of greater sensitivity that will have major consequences or impact on your wellbeing or the wellbeing of those closest to you.

In these circumstances it is important for you to go within, to find a quiet time for yourself and ask for help in making your decision. When you ask for help in this manner you are asking through the medium of prayer, for the sincerity of your question denotes that you are asking in faith that you will receive the answer. When your mind is in this quiet state, you immediately draw to you those loved ones in spirit who wish to help you due to their continued love for you and because your heart and soul are now in active supplication, radiating out love to the universal power of the Divine Father God who hears all and sees all. You will receive your answer in due time, be patient and willing to accept it when it comes.

Change the way you think

When situations in your life keep being repeated over and over again, and you are left wondering, why, then there is clearly a need for something to change. All outcomes are dependent upon your actions and your reactions, and it is up to you as best you can, to guide the situation to a positive end for all involved. There have been many times when you were, on reflection, unhappy with the way you may have handled a situation or responded to someone involved in it, and your emotions and thought processes may have got in the way of the flow. Positive or negative, your reaction was a response to the way you were thinking at the time, and this is now the time to make changes in your pattern of thinking.

Firstly, clear thought will always help you to see the situation as it is, and not what you perceive it should be. If you can be clear in your thinking, the end result can be influenced. Secondly, to remain as calm as possible can be the key to a positive outcome. The emotions can cause waves that upset the peace that you want to achieve. Give yourself the opportunity to be relaxed, in the knowledge that the outcome has already been effectively established in your mind. You have already positively influenced the conversations with those who matter, and they will act in your favour. Trust the process to work, and you will always know and feel the satisfaction that is generated within your mind. As you think, so it is and will become.

The power of thought cannot be reckoned with when used in a positive and loving way. Think yourself into wellbeing, and know that the spirit of love will always seek to be dominant if you channel it in the right way.

A new door is opening for you

At this time in your life, you are in a place of constantly seeking to change your direction, but it seems that with each attempt, your steps are thwarted and blocked at every turn. Do not despair, for the opportunities that you seek are about to enter your life, rather than you finding and locating them. Spirit are at work making the positive influences in the right places, so that those changes will become more permanent rather than just fleeting visits in your life.

We know your hearts desires and we also know what benefits these changes will bring to you, so try not to fret or think that you have been forgotten. You are at a new crossroads in your life, and this time is one of importance in your growth as a spiritual being, and the changes have to be gradual in order for them to be set in motion and to gain momentum. You will understand why and how your steps have been guided to this particular door in the way they have, and in time you will see that your patience and sometimes impatience, were all part of the process of growth and learning.

Continue to walk the path provided for you, and know that our guidance is always there with love when you need it. Keep smiling and know that we are with you always.

Make your decision

Life on earth is all about making decisions. You cannot get through the day without having to decide on some action that needs to be taken in order to accomplish or achieve something. Your actions sometimes determine a certain outcome depending on which decision you make, and it is understandable that you will opt to delay making a decision due to uncertainty about how it may affect you and those around you. When you have the best interests at heart of all those concerned, you cannot go wrong, for that loving interest will always influence your decision to become the correct one. Even if the outcome is adversely affected by outside circumstances beyond your control, you know that when you made your decision you did so with good intentions, so there is no need for you to be fearful.

When you are unsure and need guidance, connect with your heart and offer up a prayer for help in making the outcome the best one possible for all. We in spirit will hear you and will help in the best way that we can, for we are your helpers and guardians, and want only what is best for you and for your spiritual growth and wellbeing. Make your decision and have faith that whatever you decide to do, if it is done out of the desire for prosperity, your choice will bring about the changes needed for you to experience further necessary lessons for your soul's growth.

In your heart you know what to do

Sometimes in life it is hard to know for sure what action you must take for the best. On earth your sight is limited and you cannot always see what the results will be of the choices that you make. You are blessed with intuition which resides deep within your heart, and it is usually when situations become desperate that you are pushed to rely on your senses of the spiritual nature, and it is then that you will instinctively tap into this awareness to help yourself. You will at first feel at a loss as to what you should do, but when you are seemingly backed into a corner your heart always knows. Listen to its voice. If you are still and calm enough you will hear its guidance, at first just as a whisper, and as you attune yourself to its sound and how it feels, you will become accustomed to its voice every time it responds to your question of, what shall I do?

The innermost part of you in its gentleness and purity longs to lead you along the pathway of light, and when you begin to trust it, it will lead you to the right road where you will only benefit from life's fountain of rich experiences, that can only increase your future judgement of situations and needs that affect you personally. Take a deep breath now and listen to your heart.

Do not let your emotions control you

In life you are met with many situations that will cause your emotions to rise up. These emotions can vary from being very mild, to being extremely powerful and sometimes overwhelming. We are all people of varying degrees of sensitivity and will all react differently to different stimulating circumstances that will sometimes be emotive in their origin.

Take care always to keep the emotions that you feel on an even keel whenever possible. It is so easy to go along with the almost avalanche- like cascade of emotions that are being felt at any given moment and to end up in a place that you find it difficult to come back from. When you are in control of your emotions, you will sense, feel and acknowledge them but will not allow them to control you. Your actions as a result of your emotions, should bear the sign of one who knows how to temper and subdue any negative feelings that you may be experiencing by not allowing them to erupt, causing harm to both yourself and those close to you. Reactions of an emotional kind can have a physical affect on your body if they are allowed to constantly take over and rule you, and illness of mind or body can result.

Take every opportunity to keep your emotions in check, remember that you are in control as a spiritual being, with strengths that are not limited by anyone else but yourself. Gather your thoughts and remain calm and in control always, recognising the light that shines within you and the strength it contains.

It is time to take control

You often sit back and allow others to pull the strings and make decisions on your behalf, simply to keep the peace or just because it is easier to do so, and then when you find yourself on a course to a destination that you do not wish to visit, you complain or you wonder why you are in a situation that does not benefit you in any way or causes you to feel unsettled and uncomfortable.

It is time now for you to take control of this runaway train that you are on. You do not have to stay the course or feel that you have to, if you are not happy. Your life is in your control and you should not allow others to direct your life, or manoeuvre it to a place that you do not wish to be. You may hear grumblings of disagreement from those around you who are used to directing your life for you once you make the decision to steer your own boat, but don't let that stop you from being in control of the pleasures in life that are yours by right to embrace.

You are now in a place mentally where you know exactly what you want to achieve, and you know how you want to go about getting it, so now is the time to take a leap of faith, knowing that you can do and will do what is necessary to make your dreams a reality.

This is a new day for you and an opportunity for a new tomorrow and a new future to be created. We will guide your steps all the way.

It is time to express who you really are

You have been living in the shadow of others for long enough, and it is time for you to come out of those shadows into the light so that all can see who you truly are. Your light has been stifled for too long and you have forgotten the truth and the strength of your true being. You have within you the light of spirit that wishes only to shine and to express itself. You no longer have to fear that expression in case others are offended by your truth. You are who you are by design and if they do not agree with your self- expression then they will have to speak to the Great Designer who fashioned you.

Your pathway stretches out before you, beckoning your footfall so that you can meet those opportunities destined for your attention and experience. You do not need to apologise to anyone or get anyone's permission. Just take a step by deciding that today is the day that I allow myself to change my life and my direction, by expressing the truth of who I am and who I have always been.

Those who are in synchronisation with the spirit of who you are will continue to be by your side, but those who are destined for a different pathway to yours will take their leave as naturally as the leaves fall from the tree. Your new found freedom will strengthen you and give you a new voice to become at peace with yourself.

Do not hide your talent

Each and every one of us was created by the greatest Designer in the universe. We are all individuals in our own right with different personalities and diverse talents added to our character and makeup. You as an individual should never be afraid to share or express your talents, for they were given to you to enhance the lives of all those whom you share your life with, or who may just be passing through your life towards their destination and as you journey towards yours. It is important that you give others a little joy and happiness through your sharing and expressing your gifts. Do not be afraid of who you are, or fear what others may think, because by doing this you do yourself a great disservice. Someone may be in need of a gift at this particular time in their lives.

You are worthy of praise even though this is not what you seek, but you must allow yourself the privilege of growing spiritually by serving. Try to forget the triviality of self, not in any neglectful way, but in the sense that when you are serving others it is never about you, and when you focus totally on what you offer with the desire to uplift, there is not time to think about the 'you' and all your inferior complexes.

Rise above these things and share your gifts and talents, the rewards will be heart warming and will restore your faith in yourself.

Your happiness is all we care about

You may think that you are all alone in this world, but you are wrong, and even though you may sometimes feel that nobody cares about you, you are loved by many on the other side of the veil which separates the physical world from the spirit world.

We make great efforts to try and soothe you when you are in pain, or are depressed and sad and we care greatly about your welfare and your wellbeing. We do for the most part of your life go unnoticed by you, but that will never deter us from our attempts in making our loving presence felt by you. Even when you express that your imagination is running wild with the things you may see or sense, we rejoice in that acknowledgement that you felt or saw some evidence of our visits, and it brings us a step closer to you.

You are a child worthy of every effort we make to convince you that you do not walk alone, and when you are happy so are we. When you rejoice, you are not alone in your tidings of joy for there are many here who rejoice with you. Our sentiments are such that will always strive for harmony, and this we do against all the odds of what the physical world presents to us. We have no other agenda than the one of bringing love and happiness to our fellow spirit friends and loved ones on the earth, and you are no exception but our priority.

Understand that you are not an isolated island but are an oasis of potential and a fountain of love whom we enjoy being with each day.

You are entitled to happiness

Happiness is your right and your entitlement. You were not sent to this earth plane to suffer in silence or otherwise, no matter how much you may experience sadness or negativity from others. It is often the case that you get stuck in a rut which may be due to circumstances beyond your control, but this does not mean that this is now your lot in life. It does not mean that you now have to humbly accept your circumstances as being the final destination of your pathway.

There are many new paths for you yet to travel, and at this particular time in your life, this pause that seems to be taking longer than a pause should, may well be looking as if you are standing still, but gather your strength for once this temporary halt turns into a move forward, you will gather momentum and will need your strength to sustain you.

The happiness that seems to have been lacking in your life for so long, will appear from unsuspecting sources and places that you could never envisage them to be, and your entitlement to that happiness will never be questioned again by yourself or by others.

A rainbow for you

When you wake up each day, understand that there is above you a rainbow of love and protection that is with you throughout the day. It is a force that never leaves you and will be with you always. Its colours shine with vibrancy in their representation of all that is in harmony and complete, and though you may not see it, if you are still in mind you will feel it. It represents all that is positive, its colours never blurring but blending one into the other as do the opportunities and circumstances in your life.

The nature that surrounds you which is also part of your life, begets the same vibrancy of life that you can impart to your very being. Close the door to all that is negative and all that threatens to pull you down spiritually, and embrace only the light of life, the truth and the harmony which the rainbow brings, for it is the light that gives the rainbow its birth, and from which springs all things that will eventually become to you gifts of the spirit.

Let this day be the last day that ideas of doom and gloom enter your mind, for they are just shadows of the past, occurrences that have long gone and are lost in time. Bring forward your positive mind that has the strength to abolish the dark and create a future guided and protected by the rainbow of love.

When you are feeling sad I will lift your spirits

I have not gone but am by your side, especially when things in your life are threatening to overwhelm you. On these occasions your thoughts become out of control and tend to spiral down instead of up. When they spiral down it is harder for me to reach you in mind, for the light takes longer to penetrate, but I am never discouraged by this and my efforts to reach you are doubled. Think of me and I will give you hope and strength to carry on.

When the fight seems to have gone from you, just accept my love and my embrace, for I shall not leave you at a time of need. I will dry your tears; I will take your pain if you will just abandon the resistance that you put up as a wall. We can walk together as I guide you to a place of rest where you can gather your strength through the healing that I will bring for you. You will know and understand that you are not alone, for you will feel the warmth as you tremble in despair.

Pick up your feet and walk one step at a time. You will not fall or falter for we will cause you to see clearly the way ahead with a new passion and a new desire for a brighter future. We are many, and although it is me that you think of at this time, I will secure the help of others who also have your loving care in their hands and hearts. Do not be discouraged.

God has not forgotten you

As a child of the great spirit of love, please know that you are not forgotten. You are an individual soul among many, but His love for you is also individual. That does not lessen His love for you but increases it so that it can be felt only by you in a unique way. You have never been alone in this world and never shall you be in the next, but you must start to believe that you are a special being of spirit accompanied by friends of spirit and chaperoned when you are in need of guidance.

There are many in life that lose their way along the road and journey back home, and even they are not left to their troubles or abandoned, so let not your fears of loneliness encompass your mind causing you to feel as though you are isolated or forgotten. It is time for you to know the strength that you possess within. You are not a puppet on a string being manipulated to do things that you do not want to do, but are a free spirit with the desire to improve and raise yourself up against the things that try to defeat you, and these things are trials for you to overcome in victory and are always faced with the help of those unseen who encourage your determination to overcome.

You are blessed always and kept in the light of His loving care through the many helpers He has sent to shield you and protect you.

You are here to learn from your mistakes

Think of all the errors you have ever made and the valuable lessons that you have learnt from them. How naive you would now be if those lessons had never been learnt. Your life would be in much more turmoil if you were still making those some mistakes that you now know how to avoid. It does you no good spiritually or mentally to dwell on the errors of the past, for it only helps you to stand still and stagnate. The mind needs to be open to allow fresh and new ideas and knowledge to enter, but if it is full of the old carcasses of past mistakes which are made so big by your constant beating of the same drum of guilt, you will never be able to move forward.

You do not need to punish yourself in this way, for not only will stagnation of mind take place but new opportunities will pass you by unnoticed because your focus is in the wrong direction. Keep your focus ahead at all times and allow yourself to be open to new ideas that will benefit you in the future.

Don't be alarmed if a new idea looks like an old familiar error of the past, for it may just be the fear in you that is giving it a familiar identity so that you can avoid the same circumstances. You now have a renewed stance and strength of avoidance, that will guide you to be in the right place at the right time to usher in your new age of self belief.

I speak to you in unexpected ways

I know that it is sometimes hard for you to believe that although I am gone physically, I am still with you in spirit. I am still the same in personality and passion, and have the same ability to love you which has increased since leaving my physical body. In the same way that we used to communicate and converse when I was on the earth, I can still speak to you now, but I have to use the tools of the earth in which to do this since you can no longer hear my voice.

The tools that I now use are all around you. Sound is most valuable to you at present and this I can use to make my presence known. There are ways that you wouldn't normally expect me to use, such as your awareness of your surroundings. This type of communication you would normally put down to coincidence, but often they are not. When you suddenly become aware of a written word, or a sentence, it is because I have used your natural sense of awareness to reply to a question or to let you know that I am still with you. I may also use this way to guide you in decisions you have to make. You may tune in to the television or radio and hear a communication in the words that are spoken when you have asked me to give you a sign that I am with you. Listening for my voice only will limit our relationship rather than allow it to grow. There is no limit to where or how I speak to you. Open your mind and allow me to speak to you in ways that I could not do when on earth, and then we can be closer than ever before. I am still with you and my love for you continues.

Open your eyes as well as your ears

You are constantly seeking for communication with those who have left the earth plane and who now reside in the world of spirit. You do this without realising that the communication you seek is already taking place, though it goes unnoticed by you. The voice of reason that speaks to you daily is strong within you, and this in itself is a form of communication which we use to guide you in ways that can determine your future and all its benefits, but I ask you to also open your eyes of spirit to see the light that guides and often points the way for you.

It is not a physical beam of light but a light that envelops you often in a way that can be felt as a certainty of direction, a certainty of knowing that this is for me. You cannot always explain to people why you are sure or how you are sure, but you just know, and this is when the eyes of the spirit within you are open and are seeing what is being shown to you.

The vision of the earth is physical, but the vision of the spirit is sensed and felt in many ways. It is a different kind of vision, but vision nevertheless. Even the physically blind can see. You rely on your ears too much when seeking to relate to our communications, but if you let your senses and feelings become your eyes, you will see far more clearly and realise the closeness of those you love. The veil between us can then be dissolved leading to a beautiful blending of both our worlds.

Do not be afraid I come with love

There are many who still do not know the truth of continued life after physical death, and for them the pain of losing their loved ones is far more painful and emotional than it should be, to the point that their loss will sometimes leave them paralysed. It is not the way that it should be, for while it is expected that sadness will be felt, the knowledge of the truth will always lessen the pain and subdue any exaggerated and outlandish feelings and emotions which can harm those who simply do not know.

There are also those who still believe that communication is impossible once the cloak of material called the physical body has been taken off, and this ignorance of truth can prevent spiritual growth from being in their possession, but communication is a truth and we come in love always to teach and to improve life on the earth, so that at the end of physical life, the light of the world of spirit can be entered without fear and with expectations based on the truth.

There is no need for fear, because we are born out of natural love which the Creator instilled in the hearts and souls of all of His children, and that is what we come back to the earth to teach as an expression of our hearts and minds. In the future there will be many more that will have this knowledge before their passing into the life of spirit, which will of course only benefit them and those they seek to love unconditionally on the earth.

Seek more knowledge and wisdom of spirit

It is a spiritual truth that the truth shall set you free. There are many who hunger for something, and they know not what, but they know that there is a truth that exists and is needed. The soul knows that it came to the earth from a world it calls home, and it also knows that it will again return to its home after this short sojourn on the earth.

It hungers for that home and causes you to search for its truth and its wisdom. The world of spirit is filled with those who never engaged in that search while on the earth, or were indoctrinated with false teachings that held the soul in bondage and fear. You have the opportunity to seek the truth of spirit and the world that you will eventually return to, and this is the time to seek and find it.

There are many lessons to learn about the operation of the spirit laws and the operation of the world to which you will return. It is not enough to just investigate the truth of life after death and the communications that transpire between the two worlds, but there are many laws and philosophies that will help your spiritual growth and will aid you to live a life of harmony both spiritually and physically. Doctrine and truth are poles apart. One closes the mind and the other opens it wide enough to let the light of freedom in so that spiritual growth can take place.

It is up to you to seek the progress that will be yours if you listen to your soul and feed its need for light, which is truth.

Remember that you are spirit now

You are spirit now and always will be. You are not purely physical and you are not here just to adhere to the materialism of this life on earth. Your physical body contains a spirit and your spirit body contains a soul. The only permanent parts of you are your spirit body and your soul, for they will never be separated once the physical body returns to dust after its temporary job of housing the spirit and the soul is over.

Some people think that they will only become a spirit being once physical death takes place, but this is not so. You need to honour your spirit self by allowing the spiritual part of you to become the dominant party in your life. It always seeks expression in its gentle way but the physical and material parts of you, being the loudest and most domineering, drown out its voice. By learning to still the mind and make a connection with the spirit within, you can establish a rapport with the inner sanctum of your soul, this then will help you to know who you really are and will help you to move and live in a way that will bring to your soul positive benefits of spiritual accolades that do not exist in this physical world, but that are real treasures in the next.

Remember that you are responsible for your own growth, and your spiritual condition can be the difference between happiness and sadness when that transition is eventually made to the home of the spirit.

Follow your dream and make it a reality

Your dream is the desire of your soul which is waiting for the dream to be fulfilled so that it may finally find its true expression. When you have a strong desire to achieve something that you can only dream of at present, know that it can become a reality, for if you are driven by your dream to accomplish something, it may just be dormant in your heart and soul right now, but by just being there it means that you have within you an idea which can only grow, and from which all things in your future can be created.

Many things of great beauty begin as tiny seeds and quiet wishes, and great changes in the world have taken place as a result of dreams. Follow your heart and the desires of your soul, for as they are a part of your being, they must eventually be realised and can take you to places that you never thought possible both spiritually and materially. When your dream benefits others it will undoubtedly benefit you also, for what started as a mere whim can often mushroom into great feats of accomplishment.

You owe it to yourself to at least try to attain your dreams. They are not always impossible and should never be put on hold for longer than is necessary, for to do so would be a denial of your only chance to become an expression of your soul and your true self, and you will always have a feeling of being unsatisfied. Take the first step and you may be pleasantly surprised at who you truly are and the gifts that you have within you.

God will not judge you or punish you. He is Love

One of the greatest religious false teachings of this material world is that God judges and punishes His children. It is also one of the greatest fears among mankind, which causes many souls to close their minds to truth, the truth that love and our Creator are one and the same, for He is Love.

You as His child will never have to stand before Him and account for your actions on earth, because after physical death you will have an unhindered memory of all of your thoughts and actions, and the only punishment that you will encounter is the punishment that sorrow for any wrong doing will bring. You will judge your own actions in truth, and you will see yourself in truth.

This is something you do on a daily basis already. Your conscience works all the time and never sleeps. It can occasionally be ignored, but when you do this the temporary rebuttal will cause the conscience to come back stronger and louder at a later date. Cause and effect is in action at all times. It is the law. Do not fear, for you will not attend a court in the world of heaven and you will not be cast out or into any place that resembles fire or the like, for these are earthly imaginings that are not based on truth, but are taught by those who feel the need to control others through fear because their own knowledge is lacking.

Be content and comforted to know that God is Love and is merciful towards all of His children, offering unlimited spiritual progress to all who want to embrace it.

Your soul is far more important than all the materials of this world

This material world in which you live is but your temporary home. It has become to you, all that you know and your whole reality, but the fact that this is only your temporary earthly accommodation for your spirit and soul, is rarely ever thought about by you except on the occasions when loved ones have left this physical earth, and it is at those times that you will give thought to the things of a more spiritual nature. You are by nature spiritual beings living in a physical body, and this truth should be your true self expression.

The soul that came to this earth is the part of your very being that will last for ever. It is the everlasting part of you that will survive physical death along with your spirit body within which the soul is housed, and because your soul cannot die, it is far more important than any material object that exists on the earth, including your physical body which is just a temporary overcoat.

Your soul should be fed and clothed just like your physical body, for the soul can be spiritually undernourished and starved of light, which can affect your progress in the world of spirit to which you will go when you leave this earth. Truth is light, and the knowledge of spiritual truths is essential to the condition of your soul and its eventual happiness.

Educate your soul with knowledge of spiritual truths, and this will undoubtedly give you the wisdom that you require, when you eventually graduate from the nursery of earth into the school of spirit for your further education.

Take the first step; I will hold your hand

You have been in the darkness of your situation and circumstances for far too long and they have stifled your spirit. On many occasions you have wished and desired that things could change, and although you may feel that you do not have the confidence or the strength to move forward, you have within you a wealth of strength yet untapped.

The change that your heart desires to make can be achieved by you, if you will just take little steps at a time, and I will hold your hand as you take the first step. First you must make the decision that you are going to take that step. Then you must rise up and stand tall, for your circumstances have convinced you over time that you are small and insignificant, when in fact you are a strong individual who stands taller than most in spiritual stature. Then you must get your balance mentally. You may feel as though you may fall but if you focus on what you are about to achieve the strength that I bring you will not cause you to falter.

As you take that first step, I will hold your hand giving you the encouragement that you need. I am right by your side, and as you continue on your new journey, do not look back but keep your eyes on the goal straight ahead of you as you prepare to take yet another step. Before you know it you will be out of the darkness heading for the light of that brighter future you spent so long wishing for. Just take the first step.

Stay strong

We know how difficult it is for you at times to remain positive and strong when the turbulence of life seems to be endless. We understand your pain and your sadness at these times, but although the troubles you encounter seem relentless in their attack, the clouds are clearing for the sun to shine again in your life. We ask you to remain strong and although your heart might be heavy, we are gathering around you to bring you the strength of endurance for the final phase of this disturbance.

You have come far and we now help you to carry the load of uncertainty, for rest from your troubles is just around the corner although you cannot see it. Please stay strong for just a little longer, for the help that you have asked for will be forthcoming. There are many that are walking with you holding your hand and soothing your brow to release the tensions that have afflicted you for so long. Take strength from this knowledge and know that when that sun breaks through the clouds, the pathway ahead will be clear for you to see your way, and new opportunities will be yours to grasp with the surety of heart that a new beginning and a fresh outlook is upon you.

Keep your faith, for although it may have wavered from time to time, your strength of mind has seen you through to this new day that is dawning. Our love is always with you.

Do not neglect yourself

It is not your job to look after everyone else and neglect yourself. There are times when there is a need for you to say not to those who make demands upon your time and your energy. It is not always a fact that you are the only one who is able to oblige in the duty of care for others, for there are helping hands that can be called upon to share the service you provide in helping your fellow brothers and sisters. We applaud your heartfelt giving of yourself and your time, done selflessly, but we see the affect it has on your physical body and how it becomes depleted in energy.

You must not allow yourself to be at the beck and call of others at the expense of your health. You must take care of your own physical needs and your health to enable yourself to be at your best to help others. Please rest when you feel the need to, and listen to your body, it cannot function properly without its energy being replenished.

We know that the spirit within is always willing to go the extra mile for others, but even the spirit can require healing and rejuvenation when overworked. You are important to many people; please look after your wellbeing so that you have the strength to look after the wellbeing of others. We thank you for all that you do.

Continue to speak your truth

When you know the truth and speak it from your heart, it matters not that it is accepted by others. It may hurt them to hear it, but it may also help them to think and in thinking, enable them to come to the same place of truth that you are in and experience its benefits. Acceptance of truth is for some a difficult journey to embark on, and arrive at. There are many distractions and side roads that can lead off the pathway that brings happiness and contentment, but as long as the traveller on that pathway has someone to guide them and can meet people on that journey who can steer them in the right direction, then their pathway will be made easier.

You do not have to wonder or even know whether that truth will be accepted or not, your duty is just to impart that truth with the heartfelt desire to enlighten them, for when you share your truth, you give a gift which can only enhance the life of the receiver. Do not ask what they will do with the gift that you give, just give it. Do not ask how they will use it, for that is no concern of yours, but know that in speaking the truth you have helped your soul to shine its light a little more brightly, and that light has become a beacon for others who are travelling and need some direction from one who has knowledge of the terrain that lies ahead.

<u>Sometimes in your darkest hour you see the light</u>

When the darkness of life threatens to engulf you and you feel that you have lost your way, please don't give up, for even as you forage for the answers to your dilemma and the disappointments and the pain will not leave you, there are those unseen in the light who are working for your benefit and for your cause.

Try to be still, as hard as that may be for you at this time, for the stillness within you will bring you some comfort and protection against the outside turmoil that swirls and rages around you. Those who have the greatest love for you are working to bring you the help that you require. You have throughout your life been through many similar hard times, and you always survive. The light that you seek is not far away, it is just beyond the next hill which if you are steadfast, you will surmount with our help.

The dark thoughts that infiltrate your mind are preventing you from seeing the pathway clearly and prevent the light from entering. Open the door of hope just slightly and allow the sunshine of faith and joy to again be a part of you. You have the strength and the determination to overcome this period in your life, if you will just light the flame of desire for that which you want, and then you will see that the light of the future shining before you is not so very far away and is indeed the light in your darkness.

You cannot change anyone but yourself

You cannot change the way other people think or behave, as much as you would sometimes like to. It is not your responsibility, but you can change the way you think and behave and in that way, you can become the example of what you want others to be. To teach by example is the surest way to help others to look at themselves.

This is the time of your life when you feel that change is necessary and you are looking for that change outside of yourself, but your perception needs to start from the inside. You are wanting and seeking for something which is spiritual in nature and looking for it in the material things around you as well as in the people you mix with. When you begin to be dissatisfied with others it is because you are ready to improve yourself. You are ready to go to the next level of spiritual and soul development and this is why you seek to change others.

Know that within you, your soul is seeking to be closer to the Creator and when it begins to reach out to the Divine it creates a feeling of unrest within you. Take the time to be still and quiet and connect with your soul. Listen to the changes it desires to make and act upon them.

Remember that you are an eternal spiritual being who seeks to make progress in your spiritual development. Become all that your soul desires to be and you will never have to look to others for what you already have within you.

Never lose hope

Hold on to your hopes, dreams and aspirations and never let them go. Let them always be the driving force behind all that you do and keep them in focus no matter what your current situation, for they will one day become the stepping stones to the great achievements that are yours in the future. A future that was not meant to be handed to you, but was waiting for you at the top of the mountain that you determined to climb, and that you decided would be yours even through the adversities of life that fashioned and shaped you into the diamond that you were destined to become, and that you chose to claim as your own prize, like the Olympian awarded his medal for winning his race.

You know that you are worthy of all those dreams, and that only you can make them yours. You were created to succeed regardless of the opinions of others. Your own inner strength far outweighs any suggestion from others that your desires cannot become a reality, and this you have proved on many occasions.

Hold your head high and look straight ahead and decide today that no matter what the circumstances of your life, the spirit within you is as strong as it is eternal and its strength cannot be taken from you without your permission.

Please do not be angry

In the stillness of your heart there lies wisdom and knowledge, a knowledge that you can tap into at any time if you learn to be still and listen to its voice. The wisdom that is also there will guide you through many emotional moments if you allow it to rise up and govern those moments when you are unsure of what to do.

Emotions are powerful and strong but they too can be controlled if your desire to do so is strong enough, and they should not be allowed to overwhelm your desire for harmony and peace. When anger takes over it disturbs the peace of the spirit within, for it was created to grow in beauty and strength, but when negative emotions become dominant they will lead you only to misery and sadness, for once they become out of control and you lose your grip on them they will become destructive to both you and others around you.

Let go of any angry feelings that you may be harbouring, whether it is towards a person or a situation, for it will become a destructive tidal wave that you cannot stop once it gathers in strength. You can at any time command these feelings to subside and embrace again the energy of calm which will still the storm within and cause the lake of stillness within to again be a part of you.

Make this a strong desire that nothing outside of yourself can or will dictate your state of being, but know that you owe it to yourself to be in a constant state of spiritual wellbeing for your own sake.

Lightning Source UK Ltd.
Milton Keynes UK
UKOW05f1701111013

218884UK00001B/18/P